SHIFTING
TIME
AND
SPACE

The Story of Videotape

D0075397

EUGENE MARLOW
AND EUGENE SECUNDA

PRAEGER

New York
Westport, Connecticut
London

Copyright Acknowledgments

Interview with Jeannie Tasker, October 28, 1987. Used with permission of Jeannie Tasker.

Interview with Al Bond, October 28, 1987. Used with permission of Al Bond.

Interview with Steve Mulligan, November 30, 1987. Used with permission of Steve Mulligan.

Interview with Grant Williams, December 7, 1987. Used with permission of Grant Williams.

M. McLuhan, *Understanding media: The extensions of man*, New York: McGraw-Hill, 1964. Used with permission of McGraw-Hill.

Library of Congress Cataloging-in-Publication Data

Marlow, Eugene.
   Shifting time and space : the story of videotape / by Eugene
  Marlow and Eugene Secunda.
     p. cm.
   Includes bibliographical references (p.).
   Includes index.
   ISBN 0-275-93408-X (alk. paper)
    1. Video tape industry—History. 2. Video tapes—History.
I. Secunda, Eugene. II. Title.
HD9697.V542M37 1991
338.4'7621389324—dc20   90-7808

British Library Cataloguing in Publication Data is available.

Library of Congress Catalog Card Number: 90-7808
ISBN: 0-275-93408-X

First published in 1991

Praeger Publishers, One Madison Avenue, New York, NY 10010
An imprint of Greenwood Publishing Group, Inc.

Printed in the United States of America

The paper used in this book complies with the Permanent Paper Standard issued by the National Information Standards Organization (Z39.48–1984).

10 9 8 7 6 5 4 3 2 1

SHIFTING TIME AND SPACE

Contents

Tables and Figures

TABLES

FIGURES

Preface

Thirty-four years ago videotape entered America's consciousness. Starting from its first practical demonstration in a crowded hotel room in Chicago, it metamorphosed into a powerful media technology which forever altered America's sense of reality.

Shifting Time and Space was written to chronicle the metamorphosis of videotape from a media technology that was closely controlled by a handful of television executives, to a popular communications agent which has profoundly altered the way America consumes information and entertainment, transfers information, and exchanges ideas. The book evolved from our shared fascination with videotape's pivotal role in the development of modern communications systems, and its relationship to previously established forms of media.

It is this broad historical perspective of media, born and nurtured during our doctoral studies in the Media Ecology Program at New York University, that serves as a locus in the process of writing this book. While our names as authors are listed alphabetically as an elegant solution to the dilemma of prioritizing the attribution of credit, *Shifting Time and Space* is a truly balanced, collaborative effort.

Videotape has become the papyrus of modern times. Here are some of the diverse ways it is used today:

- Small children now feel totally at ease using simple camcorders to record the events of their lives.

- Brazilian tribesmen use videotape to argue their case with the government for the preservation of their ancestral homelands in the Amazon.

- Virtually every U.S. corporation uses videotape extensively as a primary communications vehicle. For example, annual reports are now being distributed to stockholders and analysts on tape, as are training programs for employees.

- During the 1989–90 television season, one of the highest rated shows on prime-time network TV was predicated on the videotaped "home movies" of thousands of home viewers (and tapers).

- The outcomes of U.S. criminal cases are increasingly determined by the availability of a videotaped record of the actual events or confessions to the police.

- Even nations or ideologies struggling to establish or maintain their sovereignty use videotape as the most persuasive vehicle of persuasion to their point of view. For example, the videotaped images of the young student confronting a column of tanks in Beijing's Tienanman Square unquestionably tipped the balance of world opinion against China's ruling regime during the student uprisings in 1989 after every major western news service put those dramatic pictures on television.

- With the exception of sports coverage, virtually everything seen on television today is initially videotaped prior to broadcast. Entertainment and news shows are taped, as are almost all commercials.

We wrote *Shifting Time and Space* to provide readers with a perspective about where videotape came from, where it is today, and where it is likely to evolve in coming years. We believe that videotape, like all technologies, will ultimately be replaced by more efficient systems. However, its contributions to the transformation of communications in the second half of the twentieth century assures its place in history. This book is an attempt to record it.

SHIFTING TIME AND SPACE

1

Shifting Time and Space

Once upon a time . . . Many children's stories begin with that phrase. Presumably, most adults do not consciously conduct their daily lives in terms of stories, much as children do in either fantasy or play. But even with cursory analysis it is observable that much of civilization is preserved, presented, and transmitted in story forms: *orally* (as in the oral tradition and conversation), *graphically* (as in books, magazines, newspapers, paintings), *filmically* (as in films), and *electronically* (as in radio and television).

Virtually all communication is a story of one kind or another, whether it's the family sitting down to a Thanksgiving dinner to talk about the week's events, the religious leader discussing some aspect of the liturgy, the company president presenting the strategic plan for the coming year, the newscaster giving the top story of the day, or the advertisement telling the story of a product's features and benefits. In one form or another, communication (whether oral, graphic, filmic, or electronic) is storytelling.

The "carrier" of the story's content (whether oral, graphic, filmic, electronic) has an impact on how the content is received, both physically and psychically. In other words, the communications technology (or medium) has an impact on the environment in which it is used and, consequently, on the people in the environment.

It is also true that when a new technology comes along it does not necessarily replace older technologies. If this were not true then we would have stopped talking a long time ago. The fact is, new technologies add capabilities to the communications environment that did not exist before. New technologies are, therefore, additive.

Moreover, all communications technologies have the ability to shift time and space. For example, when the unseen narrator says "Once upon a time . . . " time has been shifted. He is talking in the present. But he is talking about some other time, either past or future. Communications technologies shift space as well. In the opening of George Lucas' *Star Wars* the graphic reads "A long time ago in a galaxy far, far away . . . " This is but one example of a storyteller shifting us not only in time but from our present space to a different space as well.

INTRODUCING: VIDEOTAPE

Since the early part of the nineteenth century, many technological innovations have been electronic in nature: the telegraph, for example, being the first. In the twentieth century, many of our technological innovations have not only been electronic, they have also been visual in nature: television being a prime example. Even more recently, other electronic and visual (electrovisual) devices have appeared on the scene. Many are interactive in nature: the video disc, video teleconferencing, video games, personal computers, electronic word processing, satellites, multipoint distribution systems, cable television, . . . and videotape.

Since its introduction in 1956 videotape has spawned a multibillion dollar industry: in broadcasting (programing and commercials), the home video market, and the nonbroadcast television market (also known as the private television industry). Clearly, videotape has become a major carrier of a broad range of stories.

The question is: What economic and social impacts has videotape had on the American communications media landscape since its commercial introduction in 1956? In order to answer this question, we need first to take a general look at media, culture, and the shifts new media can have on culture.

MEDIA AND CULTURE

What happens when a new technology is introduced into a culture? According to such writers as Harold Innis, Marshall McLuhan, Neil Postman, and others, graphic, filmic, and electronic media create different kinds of communications environments. New media impact on older media. Moreover, according to Innis and McLuhan, communications media create environments that can be described in economic terms, for example, supply and demand, pricing, monopolies, marketing, mass production, standardization, interchangeability, technological extension.

In *Empire and Communication*, economic historian Harold A. Innis (1950), commenting on "the effects of writing in shaping the intellectual, social, economic and political life of man," (McLuhan & Logan, 1977, p. 375) writes:

> The art of writing provided man with a transpersonal memory. Men were given an artificially extended and verifiable memory of objects and events not present to sight or recollection. Individuals applied their minds to symbols rather than things and went beyond the world of concrete experience into the world of conceptual relations created within an enlarged time and space universe. . . . Writing enormously enhanced a capacity for abstract thinking. . . . Man's activities and powers were roughly extended in proportion to the increased use and perfection of written records. (pp. 10–11)

In *The Bias of Communication*, Innis (1951a) suggests that "Western civilization has been profoundly influenced by communication and that marked changes in communications have had important implications" (p. 3). Innis covers a broad range of communications media from roughly 4,000 B.C. (starting with clay, the stylus, and cuneiform script), to printing and radio. For each period he attempts "to trace the implications of the media for the character of knowledge and to suggest that a monopoly or an oligopoly of knowledge is built up to the point that equilibrium is disturbed" (pp. 3–4). He also proposes that "inventions in communication compel realignments in the monopoly or the oligopoly of knowledge" (p. 4).

Throughout the work, there is constant reference to economic fundamentals, that is, primary laws of supply and demand, the impact on media of communication, and their ultimate reflection in the character of a particular culture. For example:

> By the end of the fourteenth century the price of paper in Italy had declined to one-sixth the price of parchment. Linen rags were its chief cheap raw material. In the words of Henry Hallam, paper introduced "a revolution . . . of high importance, without which the art of writing would have been much less practiced, and the invention of printing less serviceable to mankind. . . . " It "permitted the old costly material by

which thought was transmitted to be superseded by a universal substance which was to facilitate the diffusion of the
works of human intelligence." (p. 19)

Innis also makes reference to the time and space aspects of communication media.

A medium of communication has an important influence on
the dissemination of knowledge over space and over time. . . .
According to its characteristics it may be better suited to the
dissemination of knowledge over time than over space, particularly if the medium is heavy and durable and not suited
to transportation, or to the dissemination of knowledge over
space than over time, particularly if the medium is light and
easily transported. The relative emphasis on time or space
will imply a bias of significance to the culture in which it is
imbedded. (p. 33)

Thus, in Innis' terms, time represents a concern with history, tradition, and the growth of religious and hierarchical institutions. On the
other hand, space implies the growth of empire, expansion, concern
with the present, and secular political authority. Temporal culture
is one of faith, afterlife, ceremony, and the moral order. Spatial
culture is secular, scientific, materialistic, and unbounded (p. 156).

In his review of Innis' work Daniel J. Czitrom (1982), in *Media and
the American Mind*, points out, "Obviously, in any culture both sets
of values are operative, one dominantly and one recessively. Innis saw
the rise and fall of civilizations, especially empires, in terms of a
dialectic between competing monopolies of knowledge based on the
temporal or spatial bias" (pp. 156–157).

In *Explorations in Communication*, an anthology derived from
Explorations, a journal on communications published between 1943
and 1959, Edmund Carpenter and Marshall McLuhan (1960) "explored
the grammars of such languages as print, the newspaper format and
television" (p. ix). With regard to print, McLuhan and Carpenter point
out:

The phonetic alphabet and all its derivatives stress a one-
thing-at-a-time analytic awareness in perception. This intensity of analysis is achieved at the price of forcing all else in
the field of perception into the subliminal. We win, as a result
of this fragmenting of the field of perception and the breaking down of movement into static bits, a power of applied
knowledge and technology unrivaled in human history. The

price we pay in existing personally and socially in a state of almost total subliminal awareness. (p. xi)

By way of comparison:

Postliterate man's electronic media contract the world to a village or tribe where everything happens to everyone at the same time: everyone knows about, and therefore participates in, everything that is happening the minute it happens. Television gives this quality of simultaneity to events in the global village. (p. xi)

In "Classroom Without Walls," McLuhan (1960a) expands on the economically derived "monopoly" theme advanced by Innis by comparing the use of books in the classroom to other media, such as the press, magazines, film, and television with respect to the presumed typical role of books.

The sheer quantity of information conveyed by press-magazines-film-TV-radio far exceeds the quantity of information conveyed by school instruction and texts. This challenge has destroyed the monopoly of the book as a teaching aid and cracked the very walls of the classroom so suddenly that we're confused, baffled. (p. 1)

The "standardization" issue is referenced by McLuhan (1960b) in "The Effect of the Printed Book on Language." In this article McLuhan states, "Print meant the possibility of uniform texts, grammars, and lexicons visually present to as many as asked for them" (p. 129). The concept of standardization or "interchangeability" is further articulated by McLuhan.

The explicit technology of written and especially printed codifications of language inherently favors any tendency to develop or utilize monosyllables as a source of new word formation. Everything we know about technology points to its natural bent for the replaceable part and the snug unit that can serve many roles. (p. 134)

In *The Gutenberg Galaxy*, McLuhan (1962) expands on the concept that media, that is, technologies, tend to create new human environments. "Technological environments are not merely passive containers of people but are active processes that reshape people and other technologies alike" (p. 8). Here McLuhan proposes that technologies (communications media and otherwise) have a global impact on the culture or environment in which it is placed.

In *Understanding Media: The Extensions of Man*, McLuhan (1964) refers to the space and time aspects of communications media. On the global level, McLuhan points out that after 3,000 years of explosion, by means of fragmentary and mechanical technologies,

> the Western world is imploding. . . . Today, after more than a century of electric technology, we have extended our central nervous system itself in a global embrace, abolishing both space and time as far as our planet is concerned. (p. 3)

McLuhan also contends new media displace older media in various ways. In one chapter, "The Printed Word," he compares printing with electric information.

> The book was the first teaching machine and also the first mass-produced commodity. In amplifying and extending the written word, typography revealed and greatly extended the structure of writing. Today, with the cinema and the electronic speed-up of information movement, the formal structure of the printed word, as of mechanism in general, stands forth like a branch washed up on the beach. (p. 174)

In effect:

> A new medium is never an addition to an old one, nor does it leave the old one in peace. It never ceases to oppress the older media until it finds new shapes and positions for them. (p. 174)

Later he says, "Once a new technology comes into a social milieu it cannot cease to permeate that milieu until every institution is saturated" (p. 177).

Coming full circle, McLuhan makes the connection between energy and production on the one hand, and information and learning on the other.

> Marketing and consumption tend to become one with learning, enlightenment, and the intake of information. This is all part of the electronic implosion that now follows or succeeds the centuries of explosion and increasing specialism. The electronic age is literally one of illumination. Just as the light is

at once energy and information, so electronic automation unites production, consumption, and learning in an inextricable process. (p. 350)

The economic aspects of McLuhan's thinking, perhaps an extension of Innis' professional orientation and influence, are also expressed in his statement that "technological media are staples or natural resources, exactly as are coal and cotton and oil" (p. 21).

McLuhan comments on technologies' power to seemingly create a demand for itself.

This power of technology to create its own world of demand is not independent of technology being first an extension of our bodies and senses. When we are deprived of our sense of sight, the other senses take up the role of sight in some degree. But the need to use the senses that are available is as insistent as breathing—a fact that makes sense of the urge to keep radio and TV going more or less continuously. (pp. 67–68)

The economic aspects of technology are summarized by McLuhan as follows:

Many people have begun to look on the whole of society as a single unified machine for creating wealth. . . . But the peculiar and abstract manipulation of information as a means of creating wealth is no longer a monopoly of the stockbroker. It is now shared by every engineer and by the entire communications industries. With electricity as energizer and synchronizer, all aspects of production, consumption, and organization became incidental to communications. The very idea of communication as interplay is inherent in the electrical, which combines both energy and information in its intensive manifold. (p. 354)

McLuhan continued to express his propositions in the 1967 work written with Quentin Fiore entitled *The Medium Is the Massage*, an obvious word play on his chapter "The Medium Is the Message" from the earlier *Understanding Media*. In this work, McLuhan reiterates an earlier message.

Societies have always been shaped more by the nature of the media by which men communicate than by the content of the communication. . . . The alphabet and print technology fostered and encouraged a fragmenting process, a process of specialism and of detachment. Electric technology fosters and encourages unification and involvement. It is impossible to understand social and cultural changes without a knowledge of the workings of media. (p. 8)

And further:

Media, by altering the environment, evoke in us unique ratios of sense perceptions. The extension of any one sense alters the way we think and act—the way we perceive the world. When these ratios change, men change. (p. 41)

Another author, Eric Havelock (1976), in *Origins of Western Literacy*, discusses the relationship between the development of Western culture and the invention of the Greek alphabet. Havelock contends that because of this visually symbolized standardization of oral communication (through the use of unambiguous and therefore efficient letters that distinguish between discrete vowels and consonants which, in turn, trigger instant recognition of discrete sounds), Western man was given greater freedom of novelty: science, industrialization, and the general democratization of knowledge. The effect of this new communication technology was to allow increasingly larger numbers of people to communicate through the act of reading. Moreover, by using visual symbols to represent sounds at the level of phonemes (rather than one symbol to represent whole words, a person, place, or thing), the Greek alphabet became an abstraction and allowed for greater manipulation of thought. Accordingly, the Greek alphabet contributed to the rise of Western civilization with its concomitant industrial and scientific revolutions.

Neil Postman (1979), professor of media ecology at New York University, has also analyzed the structure of communication environments. In an article entitled "The Information Environment," he posits:

Every society is held together by certain modes and patterns of communication which control the kind of society it is. One may call them information systems, codes, message networks, or media of communication; taken together they set and maintain the parameters of thought and learning within a culture. Just as the physical environment determines what the source of food and exertions of labor shall be, the information environment gives specific direction to the kinds of ideas, social attitudes, definitions of knowledge, and intellectual capacities that will emerge. (p. 234)

Further, he states:

> the means by which people communicate comprise an environment just as real and influential as the terrain on which they live. And further: that when there occurs a radical shift in the structure of that environment this must be followed by changes in social organization, intellectual predispositions, and a sense of what is real and valuable. (p. 235)

In this article, Postman gives structure to the several properties of information. For example, he states "Information, first and foremost, has form." He points out:

> The printing press, the computer, and television are not therefore simply machines which convey information. They are metaphors through which we conceptualize reality in one way or another. They will classify the world for us, sequence it, frame it, enlarge it, reduce it, argue a case for what it is like. Through these media-metaphors, we do not see the world as it is. We see it as our coding systems are. Such is the power of the form of information. (pp. 240–241)

Postman also points out information has quantity (or magnitude) and speed (or velocity). With respect to the former, the question is: How much information is there? With respect to the latter, the question is: What kind of medium is involved? "It makes a difference in what we make of the world if information moves slowly, as in oral cultures, or at the speed of light, as in electronic cultures" (p. 241).

In addition, Postman states information has direction, and it is important to observe who has access to information in the culture. In effect, "Change the form of information, or its quantity, or speed, or direction, or accessibility, and some monopoly will be broken, some ideology threatened, some pattern of authority will find itself without a foundation" (p. 248).

TECHNOLOGICAL INNOVATION AND DIFFUSION

To answer the question of what happens when a new technology is introduced into a culture, it is also important to understand the process of diffusion and evolution of technological innovation. The process of diffusion of technological innovation is described by Alvin Toffler (1970) in *Future Shock*:

> Technological innovation consists of three stages, linked together in a self-reinforcing cycle. First, there is the creative, feasible idea. Second, its practical application. Third, its diffusion through society. The process is completed, the loop closed, when the diffusion of technology embodying the new idea, in turn, helps generate new creative ideas. (p. 27)

Jean Gimpel (1976) in *The Medieval Machine* also proposes an evolutionary model of technology.

> Technological progress is cyclical, as is most of history. . . . The cycles are dependent on the close relationship between the psychological drive of a society and its technological evolution. . . . In the era of growth the curves of psychological drive and technological evolution are parallel or the society would cease to progress. But as soon as the society reaches its maturity the curves stop rising and begin to converge. The psychological drive diminishes in intensity and begins a downward movement. In the declining era the technological evolution curve falls, though not rapidly, as that of the psychological drive, because aging societies continue to invest quite heavily in military technology. (p. 240)

The evolutionary nature of technology and its impact on culture is similar in concept to that proposed for the development of science by Thomas S. Kuhn (1962) in *The Structure of Scientific Revolutions*. In this work Kuhn proposes that scientific revolutions (which he defines as "the extraordinary episodes in which that shift of professional commitments occurs" (p. 6)) occur in various stages.

The first stage is the so-called "pre-paradigm" stage characterized by "continual competition between a number of distinct views of nature" (p. 9) and "frequent and deep debates over legitimate methods, problems, and standards of solution" (pp. 47–48). The second stage in the cycle is the "first paradigm" stage during which the first paradigm "is usually felt to account quite successfully for most of the observations and experiments easily accessible to that science's practitioners" (p. 28).

The next stage Kuhn calls the "emergence of anomaly" in which "nature somehow violates the paradigm-induced expectations" (p. 52). The emergence of a mounting number of "anomalies" results in "crisis" phase. Says Kuhn, "a crisis may end with the emergence of a new candidate for paradigm and with the ensuing battle over its acceptance" (p. 84). Thus, the crisis stage is followed by the "new paradigm" stage during which several things occur; for example, "Though the world does not change with a change of paradigm, the scientist afterward works in a different world" (p. 121). Further, Kuhn observes, "though he may previously have employed them differently, much of his language and most of his laboratory instruments are still the same as they were before" (p. 129).

Kuhn's model of the "scientific revolution" has the "evolutionary" model concept in common with Toffler's view of the diffusion of technology and Gimpel's "technological progress" view of society. Kuhn's model also echoes those views of media and culture expressed by Innis and McLuhan. For example, Innis' discussion of "monopolies of knowledge" disturbed by the introduction of new media is echoed by Kuhn's idea of existing scientific paradigms challenged by the accumulation of anomalies that lead to crisis and finally a new paradigm. When Kuhn talks about scientists changing their perception of the world when new paradigms are evolved (even though the world has not changed), he reiterates in the "scientific" context what McLuhan (1964) discusses when the latter says, "The effects of technology do not occur at the level of opinions or concepts, but alter sense ratios or patterns of perception steadily and without resistance" (p. 18).

The concept of equilibrium voiced by both Innis and McLuhan is expressed by Kuhn in the term "anomalies," that is, a scientific paradigm (monopoly of knowledge) may exist for a time, but sooner or later anomalies appear and cause disequilibrium (crisis) which leads to the development of a new paradigm (a new monopoly of knowledge). McLuhan refers to the "translating" effect of technologies; that is, "All media are active metaphors in their power to translate experience into new forms" (p. 57). One cannot help but conclude that the development of new scientific instruments (technology) helped (or forced) scientists to deal with anomalies and caused the development of new paradigms: the telescope helped change our view of the universe and the church; the microscope, our perception of medicine and ourselves.

While the writings of Innis, McLuhan, Havelock, Postman, Gimpel, and Kuhn provide a framework in which to attempt to understand the impact of technology and diffusion of technological innovation on culture, empirical studies provide another way of understanding the process.

Everett M. Rogers (1976), a leading writer in the field of technological diffusion, has pointed out, [in 1976] there are over 2,700 publications about the diffusion of innovations, including about 1,800 empirical research reports and 900 other writings. The amount of scientific activity in investigating the diffusion of innovations has increased at an exponential rate (doubling almost every two years) since the revolutionary paradigm appeared 32 years ago, as Kuhn's (1962) theory of the growth of science would predict. (p. 291)

Yet despite the extent of research in this area, another leading author in this field, Bela Gold (1981), points out, "it would seem desirable that future diffusion research concentrate more sharply on: identifying the effects of successive improvements on the technological capabilities and limitations of particular innovations" (p. 269).

SUMMARY

Based on an analysis of the abovementioned writers, we can derive various observations that lead to implications regarding the introduction and diffusion of a new technology into a culture:

1. dominant media (technologies) create knowledge empires that ultimately go into disequilibrium;
2. technologies have a bias toward either time or space;
3. technologies create total environments that are not necessarily definable by the content of the technology;
4. technologies create a demand for themselves;
5. a dominant technology creates organizational changes in a culture;
6. the diffusion of a technology into a culture takes time and the process is evolutionary;
7. the practitioners of a particular technology evolve their models, that is, paradigms, of how a technology should be applied;
8. refinements of the technology refine the models of use on the part of the practitioners.

It is in the context of these observations that the story of videotape is presented.

2

The Technology: Magnetic Recording and Videotape

To better understand the story of videotape technology and its reported use in the broadcasting, home video and nonbroadcast contexts, we will first survey developments in the technology itself.

EARLY DEVELOPMENTS: 1893–1946

In 1893 the Danish electrician Valdemar Poulsen successfully demonstrated a crude recording device; it used wire to store magnetic impulses that could reproduce sound. He was given British and Danish patents in 1898 and a U.S. patent for his "telegraphone" in 1900. In 1918 Leonard F. Fuller was issued an American patent covering the use of high frequency current for the "erasure" of magnetic recordings (Lindsay 1977, p. 43). In 1927 a British patent was filed by Boris Rtcheouloff proposing that Poulsen's telegraphone for sound recording could be adapted to record a television signal on magnetic material (Abramson, 1955).

Further developments in magnetic recording came, though, in Germany when Dr. Fritz Pfleumer received German patents in 1928 covering the application of magnetic powders to paper or plastic backing media. In that same year Allgemeine Elektrizitats Gesellschaft (AEG) and BASF, both German companies, worked on developing this concept. AEG carried on a project resulting in a product to be known as the "Magnetophon" (Lindsay, 1977, p. 43).

In 1934 the world's first magnetic tapes were manufactured in Germany, fifty in all, each 1,000 meters long. By 1939 the number had risen to 12,000; in 1944 to 86,000; all produced exclusively for German radio broadcasting stations ("Forty-three Years," 1977, p. 20). In 1938 the German Reichs-Rundfunk-Gesellschaft adopted the Magnetophon and magnetic tape as the future standard for radio broadcast recording in Germany (Lindsay, 1977, p. 43). In 1944, the Minnesota Mining and Manufacturing Company (3M) of the United States began experiments on magnetic tape coatings guided by Dr. Ralph Oace in conjunction with requests made by the Brush Development Company (*Happy 25th Birthday*, n.d.).

It was at the end of World War II that the transplantation of magnetic recording technology from Germany to the United States took place. John T. Mullin, a U.S. Army electronic specialist, and a Lieutenant Spickelmeyer were sent to Germany to look into reports the Germans had been experimenting with high frequency energy as a means to jam airplane engines in flight. While on this mission, Mullin encountered the Magnetophon. He shipped two Magnetophons to Fort Monmouth, New Jersey, for the U.S. Army. He took two other machines and sent them home to San Francisco. In early 1946 Mullin reassembled the Magnetophons and rewired them (with A.C. bias) with American parts (Mullin, 1976, pp. 62–64).

POST–WORLD WAR II

In May 1946, Mullin (p. 64) gave a demonstration of his reassembled Magnetophon at a meeting of the Institute of Radio Engineers (now the Institute of Electrical and Electronics Engineers) in San Francisco. In the audience was Harold Lindsay, who a few months later was retained by the Ampex Corporation. Ampex had been making aircraft motors during the war but was now looking for a new product, preferably in professional sound.

In June 1947, Mullin was invited to give a demonstration of his reassembled Magnetophon for Bing Crosby. The NBC radio network would not let Crosby do recordings for his radio program. Crosby took a year off and returned with Philco as his sponsor on the ABC network in the fall of 1947. ABC and Philco agreed to let him prerecord his programs (he had been looking for an alternative to the disc recordings of the day). Mullin went to work recording Crosby on tape for the 1947–48 season. This marked the first professional broadcast use of magnetic-tape recording and playback in America! (pp. 64–65).

The Magnetophones were the prototypes used by the Ampex Electric Corporation, which was also retained by Bing Crosby Enterprises in April 1948, to develop the magnetic audiotape recorder the company subsequently marketed. Thus, later in 1948, Ampex became the first company to introduce a successful American audiotape recorder (Schubin, 1986, p. 50). This work in the magnetic *audiotape* field ultimately led Ampex, until then a manufacturer of aircraft motors, to become established as the pioneer and dominant force in the early genesis of the *videotape* recorder (Mullin, 1976, pp. 62–67).

In April 1948, the ABC radio network began large-scale use of 3M Magnetic tape and Ampex Model 200s to record, delay, and rebroadcast network radio shows to compensate for daylight savings (*Tape That Takes Pictures*, n.d., p. 1).

Credit for the first major company to start serious development of videotape recordings goes to RCA. On September 27, 1951, David Sarnoff, then head of RCA, asked for three presents for his fiftieth anniversary in radio (which was to be five years later): (1) an electronic air conditioner; (2) a lightweight picture recorder that would record video signals off television; and (3) inexpensive tape (Gerson, 1981, p. 54).

RCA Laboratories, then led by Alexander Zworykin, had begun experimenting with videotape shortly after the end of World War II (Atwan, Orton & Vesterman 1978, p. 330). The RCA team demonstrated its system for the first time on December 1, 1953, but the complexity of this videotape recorder suggested the machine was still not ready to be utilized in the professional market (Abramson, 1955, p. 253). A nineteen-inch reel of one-half-inch-wide tape was required to record only a quarter-hour program (Adams, 1956).

The winner in the race to develop a videotape recorder was, however, Ampex. In October 1951 (the same year and about a month later than RCA had started work on its videotape recorder), Alexander Poniatoff, head of Ampex, and two of his top technical aides agreed that a relatively small sum of money should be appropriated for the purpose of investigating a rotating head approach to recording on magnetic tape (Ginsburg 1981). That same year the Electronic Division of Bing Crosby Enterprises gave its first demonstration of a videotape recorder in black-and-white. The device had twelve heads and utilized an exposed reel-to-reel format, as distinguished from the enclosed format of the videocassette recorder, which evolved later (Abramson, 1973, p. 189).

Gould (1956) described the videotape recording process as follows:

> In television recording, the electronic camera changes the variations in light, which compose a picture, into a long train of electronic impulses. These impulses, representing the dark and bright parts of the picture, act on the tape in the same way as the impulses representing the variations in sound.

When the tape is played back, the impulses created by the magnetic particles can be led on wires to the picture receiving tube
or a transmitter. It is the picture tube's job to change the electrical impulses back into the variations of light and recompose
the scene as picked up originally by the cameras. (p. 13)

This videotape recorder was developed by Ampex in response to
Crosby's desire—in order to devote more time to his golf game—for
liberation from the time-consuming demands inherent in the live production of network television shows. It was the same motivation that
had inspired Crosby to pioneer the professional use of audiotape
recording when network radio was the dominant broadcast medium.
He had wanted the freedom to broadcast at his convenience, which
had not necessarily been that of his audience or the network. At that
time going on the air "live" was considered the only professionally
acceptable method of radio programing (Sterling & Kittross, 1978,
p. 252).

THE FIRST PRACTICAL VIDEOTAPE RECORDER

By 1956 the Ampex team had successfully developed a commercially
viable quadraplex videotape recorder using 3M two-inch-wide tape.
The 900 pound machine was inaugurated at the National Association
of Radio and Television Broadcasters (NARTB) Show in Chicago in
April of that year (*Happy 25th Birthday* n.d.).

The first prototype video recorders were shown to some 200 CBS-
TV affiliates gathered at the NARTB. The tape ran at a speed of fifteen inches per second (ips) past a magnetic head assembly which
rotated at a high rate of speed (Abramson, 1973, p. 189). The recorder
was a bulky console with fourteen-inch reels. It sold initially for
$75,000 per unit and functioned only in black-and-white (Sterling &
Kittross, 1978, p. 321).

Ampex's management projected sales of only thirty units over a
four-year period. During the first week of sales, however, the company took orders for eighty videotape recorders (Scherick, 1987, p.
63). Ampex earned more than $4 million in sales before the NARTB
meeting ended. In the ensuing four years, Ampex sold 600 videotape
recorders, two-thirds of which were bought by the three major television networks (Sterling & Kittross, 1978, p. 321). The Ampex system
was a technical and commercial success because it solved a problem
that had plagued previous developers: it reduced the amount of tape
required to record even a short sequence.

For example, RCA engineers had a workable videotape system, but
it consumed tape so quickly that more than a mile of tape was needed

for a four-minute recording. The RCA system, which was cumbersome and hard to use, moved a one-half-inch-wide strip of magnetic tape across a "stationary" tape head at a rate of twenty miles per hour (or thirty feet per second). Furthermore, the engineer who ran the system had to wear heavy leather gloves, which he used as brakes, to stop and rewind the machine (Lardner, 1987, p. 56).

Compared to the unwieldy RCA equipment, the Ampex system was dramatically more efficient. It was developed by a fourteen-man team—led by Ampex's chief engineer, Charles Ginsburg—that worked under top secret conditions for two and one-half years ("TV Tape Ready," 1956). Called the "transverse scanning system," the Ampex unit utilized a moving head and much wider magnetic tape—two inches—than RCA's unit. Instead of moving in a straight line down the length of the tape, as in the RCA system, the signal was recorded in a zigzag manner across the tape's surface. The head moved at a much slower speed—15 ips—which allowed the recording of considerably more material on a smaller reel. Additionally, Ampex used an FM audio format that provided sound quality superior to the AM format used in previous versions (Lardner, 1987, pp. 57–59).

The Ampex VR-1000 system was also well received by broadcasters because it allowed the television networks to air the same show at the same "clock time" throughout the country ("Birth of a New Era" 1956, p. 1). This factor is a clear example of the "time shifting" characteristic of the medium which ultimately found its way into the time shifting concept promulgated by the Japanese when they first started to market consumer versions of the technology.

MODIFICATIONS TO THE TECHNOLOGY: 1957–1986

For the next fourteen years, almost all videotape recorder design was based on Ampex's system, which was the cornerstone concept for helical-type videotape recording (a method in which video information is placed on the tape at a slant). In the ensuing three decades or so, however, videotape technology went through various developments, as the technology chronology in Table 2.1 depicts.

ANALYSIS

Since 1956 the use of videotape technology in broadcast television in the United States has indeed grown. As the figures in Table 2.2 indicate, there was, on a percentage basis, an enormous growth in the number of adopters between 1960 and 1970. While between 1970 and 1975 the rate of growth slowed considerably, between 1975 and 1980 the rate of growth almost doubled.

Table 2.1
Modifications in Videotape Technology

1957	Ampex introduces a color conversion kit for the VR-1000 ("10 Years of Video Tape Recording," 1966, p. 228).
1958	The introduction of electromechanical editing (<u>Happy 25th Birthday to Video Tape</u>, n.d.).
1959	Ampex provides first mobile VTR unit (<u>The Changing Picture in Video Tape</u>, 1959, p. 17).
1959	3M reduces rejection of videotape stock by users to 1 percent (Bennett, 1980, p. 6).
1959	The Society of Motion Picture and Television Engineers (SMPTE) establishes standards for the manufacture of videotape recorders (Abramson, 1973, p. 191).
1959	The Toshiba Company demonstrates the VTR-1 single head helical scan videotape recorder (Abramson, 1973, p. 191)
1960	Ampex introduces "Amtec": a time base error correction device (Abramson, 1973, p. 190).
1960	Ampex announces "intersync," a device which allowed the integrated use of other studio equipment, thus allowing for cuts, dissolves, and special effects in videotape recording (Abramson, 1973, p. 190).
1961	Victor Company of Japan introduces a two-head color helical scan videotape recorder ("Two-Head Color VTR," 1961, p. 21).
1961	RCA introduces a fully transistorized recorder, the VTR-22 ("Videotape," 1981).
1962	Ampex introduces "Editec" which allows machine-to-machine electronic editing, as opposed to the former, by hand, electromechanical editing ("10 Years of Video Tape Recording," 1966, p. 228).
1963	3M introduces a dropout compensator, a device which electronically replaces pieces of tape that have "dropped out" ("Videotape," 1981).
1964	Ampex introduces the VR-2000 a transistorized color high band recorder (Abramson, 1973, p. 190).
1965	Sony introduces the 1/2-inch (helical-scan) CV-2000, the first so-called "consumer" VTR format (Schubin, 1976, p. 55).

Table 2.1 (continued)

1965   Helical scan tape size drops to 1/2 inch and the price of this format size VTR drops to the $1-$3,000 range (McCabe, 1971, p. 46).

1966   Westel Company of San Mateo, California, announces the first portable back-pack (Abramson, 1973, p. 192).

1967   Ampex introduces a battery powered VTR, the VR-3000 (Abramson, 1973, p. 191).

1969   Sony announces the 3/4-inch videocassette (Abramson, 1973, p. 196).

1969   The Japanese, under the sponsorship of the VTR Committee of the Electronic Industries Association of Japan (EIAJ), agree on can standards for helical scan format VTRs (Winslow, 1976, p. 29).

1971   The SMPTE introduces time code--making computer-assisted electronic editing possible (<u>Happy 25th Birthday to Video Tape</u>, n.d.).

1971   Sony begins marketing the 3/4-inch videocassette in the United States (McCabe, 1971, p. 49).

1971   The introduction of Super High Band VTRs and videotape (Roizen, 1975/1976, p. 21).

1975   Sony introduces the 1/2-inch Betamax format in the United States (Lyons, 1976, p. 209).

1977   RCA introduces the 1/2-inch VHS format in the United States ("RCA's Home VTR Decision," 1977, p. 12).

1980   Sony demonstrates the first consumer camcorder (Schubin, 1986, p. 57).

1981   First professional camcorders shown by Panasonic, RCA, and Sony (Schubin, 1986).

           First satellite transponder auction at Southeby Parke Bernet in New York (Schubin, 1986).

1982   122 companies begin working on standardization of 8mm VTR (Schubin, 1986).

           Bosch and Hitachi demonstrate 1/4-inch camcorders (Schubin, 1986).

           First personal-computer-controlled character generator, Chyron VP-I (Schubin, 1986).

19

Table 2.1 (continued)

1983   Last National Association of Broadcasters (NAB)
            show with a quadruplex exhibit
            Quantel shows first print-typeface video
            character generator (Schubin, 1986).

            Sony's BVH-2500 is the first variable speed
            video recorder (Schubin, 1986).

1984   Quantel demonstrates first no-moving parts digital
            video recorder (Schubin, 1986).

            Sony markets first high definition
            television (HDTV) VTR (Schubin, 1986).

            8mm video introduced in the United States
            (Schubin, 1986).

1985   Panasonic introduces the MII VTR format
            (Schubin, 1986).

            GEC/McMichael introduces the first "flyaway"
            video satellite uplink (Schubin, 1986).

1986   First digital VTRs sold by Ampex and Sony
            (Schubin, 1986).

            Hitachi introduces 8mm professional
            camcorder (Schubin, 1986).

Table 2.2
Number of VTRs in Use at Broadcast/Educational Stations

YEAR	STATIONS	% CHANGE
1960	429	N/A
1965	1,059	+147
1970	2,508	+137
1975	3,466	+ 38
1980	6,156	+ 78

Sources: *TV Digest*, 1960, p. 359; *TV Factbook*, 1965, pp. 30c–34c,m 1969, pp. 26a–52a, 1974, pp. 30a–42a, 1980, pp. 40a–53a. Reprinted with permission of TV Digest.

However, the 1981–1988 period seems to offer some significant technological changes. Part of the rationale for examining the 1981–1988 period as a distinct period of technological development in terms of television in general is found in Edwin Diamond's (1982) work *Sign Off: the Last Days of Television*. In his introduction, Diamond defines

1955–1980 as the period of "traditional" television, with the period subsequent to 1980 as a "new era."

> In May 1981 RCA, parent corporation of the National Broadcasting Company, announced it was going into the cable television business. Thus RCA became the last of the big three broadcasting entities to enter the growing field of cable programming suppliers, or software makers. Both American Broadcasting Company and the Columbia Broadcasting System had earlier begun corporate ventures into cable programming for the cable-system operators in the United States. ABC Arts, a cultural cable service, planned to be on air—or on-line—in the late fall of 1981, followed by ABC Beta, billed as a cable service for women. By early 1982, too, CBS Cable promised to be transmitting a cultural service.
>
> RCA's belated crossover from traditional broadcasting technology to the new, wired technology of cable is as good a date as any to mark the end of the present era of television in the United States and the birth of a new era. (pp. ix—x).

Cable television's impact on the broadcasting industry seems to have reached a critical mass in the early 1980s. According to the National Cable Television Association, cable penetration of television households in the United States (with respect to basic cable) reached 25.3 percent by February 1981 (National Cable Television Association, 1986, p. 1). By the end of 1989 penetration was over 56 percent.

The use of satellites also seems to have reached a significant critical mass in the early 1980s. According to the *1985 World Satellite Almanac: The Complete Guide to Satellite Transmission and Technology* (Long, 1985):

> During the past four years, the cost of both commercial and home satellite receiving systems has fallen dramatically while overall quality has increased by leaps and bounds. This has given rise to many new uses of the technology.

Further:

> Today, satellites transfer most long-distance telephone calls, beam prime-time network TV programs to affiliates nationwide, link regional offices of multinational businesses with corporate headquarters, and provide access to more than 100 channels of TV programming to thousands of cable TV affiliates and millions of home satellite TV owners. (p. 56)

Presuming "during the past four years" means from 1985, then the period pointed to by the author begins in 1981. It is also interesting to note the author's use of the word "access"—a significant characteristic of the diffusion of the videotape technology in both the broadcast, home video, and corporate contexts.

The home video (or home VCR) market also appears to have reached critical mass in the early 1980s with respect to penetration of television households. According to the February 1, 1982, issue of *Television Digest*, the combination of discounted prices for videocassette recorders and availability of relatively new films on tape triggered a massive increase in videocassette recorder sales in 1981. With retail prices sliding down to about $500 per unit, sales increased more than 69 percent, resulting in 1,361,000 units sold to U.S. dealers. By the end of 1981, videocassette recorders were in 26 percent of all television households in the United States (*Television Digest*, 1982, p. 13). In 1986 the Electronics Industry Association reported 13 million videocassette recorders were sold to dealers and it was believed close to 50 percent of all American television households would have at least one unit by the end of the year ("Slow Motion," 1987).

All in all, the 1981–1989 period saw the significant market penetration of cable television and home videocassette recorders, the advent of smaller home video formats for both cameras and recording, the introduction of high definition television, computers for the creation of graphics at an accessible cost, and greater accessibility to the use of satellites. Looking back, then, at the technology chronology, which modifications and events in those years were significant in increasing the number of adopters? Several key events in those years point to two factors upon which the diffusion of the technology depends: standardization and portability.

Apart from the commercial introduction of the technology in 1956, the next most significant event took place in 1959 when the SMPTE developed standards for the technology. This event had the effect of allowing any manufacturer, in addition to Ampex and RCA, to enter the marketplace and manufacture the machine. In a sense, this standardization lent support to the technology's accessibility by larger numbers of adopters.

The next significant event took place in that same year, when Toshiba demonstrated the one-head helical scan format. The significance of this technological development is that the helical scan format (as opposed to the transverse format of the Ampex and RCA VTRs) requires a less speedy videotape transport, resulting in an overall less expensive machine and the potential for greater portability. (It should be noted Toshiba was not the first company to develop this kind of VTR format. On June 30, 1953, a German engineer by the name of

Eduard Schueller, the inventor of the first "ringhead" that made the Magnetophon possible, working in Hamburg for AEG Telefunken, filed for a patent covering a two-head helical scan recorder that is almost identical in concept to a few of the machines that were later produced in America, Japan, and Germany.) (Roizen, 1976, p. 21).

From these early developments in helical scan VTR technology later developments follow: the introduction of two-head helical scan color videotape recorder in 1961; the introduction of one-half-inch reel-to-reel machines in 1965; and the introduction of the three-quarter-inch U-matic videocassette in 1971 by Sony. This latter development allowed potential adopters even greater access to the technology. Because the tape was enclosed in a box a technician was no longer required, since anyone could put the tape into the machine, either for recording, editing, or playback.

The standardization issue was again relevant in the late 1960s when EIAJ standards were introduced for helical scan machines. These standards provided a common framework for the manufacture of machines, and thus the interchangeability of tapes among different machines of different manufacture.

Another important development, technologically speaking, which made the technology more accessible and, therefore, increased the number of adopters, was portability. The introduction of transistorization made these machines smaller and lighter and more portable (*Happy 25th Birthday* n.d.). And the development of smaller camera tubes (Abramson, 1973) made cameras smaller and more portable. These developments, together with the introduction of the three-quarter-inch videocassette and the half-inch Beta and VHS formats (Gerson, 1981, p. 54) in the mid-1970s, made helical scan VTRs that much more portable. Since then, manufacturers have introduced a portable one-inch type C helical scan format VTR which allows videographers to record a state-of-the-art broadcast quality signal (Bunyon, Grummond & Watson, 1978, p. 7).

The portability factor is reflected in the number of mobile VTRs extant between 1970 and 1980 (see Table 2.3).

Table 2.3
Number of Reported Mobile VTRs at Broadcast/Educational Stations

Year	Number
1970	476
1975	825
1980	1,880

When compared to the growth of studio-bound VTRs for the same period, the portability factor takes on an even greater significance (see Table 2.4).

As the figures in Table 2.5 show, the relative growth of mobile VTRs is greater than the growth of studio-bound VTRs. From another point of view, the growth of VTRs, particularly in the mobile area, is particularly striking when mobile VTRs are seen as a proportion of all VTRs.

It seems clear that portability of equipment is a significant factor in the increasing number of units of technology and, presumably, the number of adopters; to put it another way, the portability factor allows for a greater number of adopters that might not have existed were it not for the developments in the technology.

The case for videotape technology's adoption in the broadcast context in the United States is clear, particularly from the point of view of number of machines in use. We also see a similar pattern for the use of the medium in the home video and nonbroadcast contexts. Moreover, if standardization and portability are important issues with respect to potential adopters' access to a particular technology, then should there not also be some relation(s) between developments in videotape technology and the reported use contexts? We shall explore each market for videotape technology in turn to attempt to answer this question.

Table 2.4
Number of Reported Studio-Bound/Mobile VTRs

Year	VTRs	% Change	VTRs	% Change
1970	2,032	NA	476	NA
1975	2,641	+30%	825	+73%
1980	4,276	+52%	1,880	+128%

Table 2.5
Total VTRs

Year	No. of Total VTRs	% Mobile VTRs
1970	2,508	18.9
1975	3,466	23.8
1980	6,156	30.5

3

Television Viewing Patterns in the United States

It would be difficult to comprehend the degree to which the introduction of videotape technology shaped the commercial U.S. broadcast television industry without understanding television's origins, beginning with radio in the 1920s. For it was in the roots of radio that the fundamental elements of television's organization and growth were formed and continue to this day.

ORIGINS

Robert Saudek, former president of the Museum of Broadcasting, said the foundation of the U.S. broadcasting system was formed in the 1920s and has not changed fundamentally to the present (Long, 1979, p. 12). The basis for modern network broadcasting was created in the United States by the American Telephone & Telegraph Company (AT&T) in February 1922, when the company proposed that thirty-eight radio broadcasting stations be linked by AT&T long-distance telephone lines. The stations would each be charged a fee by AT&T and would be encouraged, in turn, to sell for commercial purposes the air time they had available. The commercial aspects of the proposal were condemned by many in the press, some of whom may have been anticipating unwanted competition for advertisers' dollars. Herbert Hoover, then U.S. secretary of commerce, echoed this negative sentiment, stating, "[It is] inconceivable that we should allow so great a possibility for service . . . to be drowned in commercial chatter" (Barnouw, 1978, p. 15).

The company launched its first toll station (WEAF) in New York City on August 16, 1922, and twelve days later aired the first radio commercial on that station. It was a message promoting a New York real estate development. This commercial was ten minutes long and cost the realtor $50. In 1923 AT&T launched a second toll station (WCAP in Washington, D.C.) and connected it by cable to WEAF in New York, thereby initiating network broadcasting or "chain broadcast," as it was called by AT&T (pp. 10–19).

THE RADIO NETWORKS ARE FORMED

AT&T was ultimately pressured by the federal government to divest itself of its radio network, which had rapidly grown to twenty-six stations. In 1926 the stations were all sold to RCA, which formed a subsidiary, NBC, to operate the chain. NBC's first president was David Sarnoff.

In 1927 the Columbia Phonograph Broadcasting System bought sixteen stations from a failing company, United Independent Broadcasters, and went into competition with NBC. That year, the Paley family, wealthy Philadelphians in the cigar business, invested in the struggling new company and shortened its name to the Columbia Broadcasting System (CBS). In 1928, 27-year-old William S. Paley became president of CBS.

The Mutual Broadcasting System was formed in 1934 by four independent commercial radio stations located in major U.S. cities (Long, 1979, pp. 32, 33). The success of the first NBC network led RCA to create a second NBC network in 1927. It called one the "red network;" the other the "blue network." These two chains were successfully operated by NBC until 1943, when the Federal Communications Commission (FCC) enacted a new set of regulations aimed at reducing the power of the older networks. When these new regulations were supported by the Supreme Court, RCA was forced to divest itself of one of its networks. It sold the blue network to Edward J. Noble, who then renamed it the American Broadcasting Company (ABC) (Head & Sterling, 1987, pp. 82, 83).

The U.S. broadcasting network system was created as a programing distribution system that exploited the availability of the era's newly developed technology. However, the first networks were not originally intended to be significant moneymakers in their own right.

Instead, they were initially created as a public service and a method of motivating potential audiences to buy radios. Broadcasting was considered by RCA to be a minor but necessary expense to generate consumer interest in, and demand for, radio equipment (Long, 1979, p. 22). It was not until the CBS network began to pose a significant competitive threat to NBC's two networks—and the onset of the Depression following the stock market crash of 1929—that the networks abandoned all pretense of altruism and openly embraced advertising and commercialism as the means of economic survival (Bergreen, 1980, pp. 6, 7).

The effects of the Depression initially slowed the growth of network radio but ultimately benefited it, as economically squeezed audiences reduced their theater and motion picture attendance and stayed at home to listen to the radio. Barnouw (1975) noted that a destitute family would surrender its refrigerator or furniture before abandoning its radio. For millions of poor Americans, radio was the only connection with the outside world. Stars of vaudeville and the theater migrated to network radio, establishing broad popularity and gaining dedicated weekly listeners. And daytime dramatic serials found enormous audiences that incorporated network radio listenership into daily living. As network radio created listening habits among a vast portion of the American public, advertisers began transforming it into a potent sales vehicle and a new mass selling medium was created (pp. 72, 73).

NETWORK RADIO BECOMES DOMINANT MASS MEDIUM

Soon after network radio emerged as a mass medium, advertisers and their advertising agencies began to shape the networks' growth as programers, as well as by providing financial support. Advertising agencies became expert at designing shows that would best fit the interests of their clients' target audiences. By the early 1930s, a small number of major advertising agencies were producing most of the nation's favorite network radio programs, skillfully associating hit programs—featuring such stars as Jack Benny and Eddie Cantor—with their clients' products. Network radio proved increasingly effective for marketers of mass-produced products, while selling techniques became more sophisticated and more aggressive. By the mid-1940s, network radio had become a primary advertising medium for national advertisers and the programing was largely a product of the advertising industry (Heighton & Cunningham, 1976, pp. 10–12).

By 1950, 95 percent of all American families owned a radio (Sterling & Kittross, 1978, p. 333). Network radio earned its greatest revenues in 1949, with total annual advertiser expenditures amounting to $203 million. By comparison, total network television-advertiser expenditures for that year came to only $30 million. Average daily radio use peaked in 1943 at four hours and forty-three minutes (Sterling, 1984, pp. 83, 220).

THE ROLE OF NETWORK AFFILIATES

While the radio networks were the clear symbols of ultimate broadcast power to the public, their very existences depended on their abilities to maintain strong and mutually profitable relationships with their affiliated stations. The prosperity of the networks was completely dependent on gaining and maintaining the cooperation of hundreds of independently owned radio stations, situated throughout the United States, that chose to affiliate themselves with one or another of them. These affiliated stations, in return for giving a network most of their programing and advertising air time, received direct compensation from ABC, CBS, NBC, or Mutual (another early radio network). They also had the opportunity to sell additional advertising time independently to national and local advertisers. By broadcasting the same show simultaneously to a large national audience, a network provided major advertisers with the most efficient and timely sales tool devised up to that time. The larger the audience, the more the network could charge for each sponsored message. The networks, based in New York City, may have been "the motor" (Brown, 1979, p. 13) that drove the system, but the affiliates blanketing America with their local radio signals were the indispensable distributors of the networks' programing and national advertising messages. It was a symbiotic relationship that formed the basis for the creation of the television networks. (Table 3.1 shows network radio station affiliates 1927–1951.)

THE BEGINNINGS OF THE TELEVISION NETWORKS

Even as network radio grew into a powerful and commercially successful force in America's social and economic life in the 1930s, its managements were preparing for the technological communications breakthrough that would build on and ultimately succeed network radio.

As early as the 1930s, commercial television had been recognized as a workable media technology. RCA, a leader in television's development in the United States, installed an experimental television studio in New York City's Empire State Building in 1932. Broadcast television, as a

Table 3.1
Number of Network Radio Affiliates, 1927–1951

Year	Total AM Stations	Total Network Affiliates	%
1927	681	44	6
1928	677	69	10
1929	696	107	15
1930	618	131	21
1931	612	151	25
1932	604	170	28
1933	599	179	30
1934	583	184	32
1935	585	188	32
1936	616	226	37
1937	646	296	46
1938	689	359	52
1939	722	396	55
1940	765	454	59
1941	831	509	61
1942	887	558	63
1943	910	620	68
1944	910	694	76
1945	919	874	95
1946	948	881	93
1947	1,062	1,029	97
1948	1,621	1,104	68
1949	1,912	1,132	59
1950	2,086	1,170	56
1951	2,232	1,210	54

Source: C.H. Sterling, *Electronic media: A guide to trends in broadcasting and new technologies, 1920–1983*. New York: Praeger, (1984), p. 12. Reprinted with permission of Praeger.

practical mass medium, was introduced to an astonished American public at the New York World's Fair in 1939. RCA and other companies involved in the manufacture of radios for home use were actively preparing to repeat, with television, the pattern of success they had experienced with network radio. They were planning to offer exciting programing that would stimulate American consumers to purchase television receivers. RCA, CBS, and others also foresaw the enormous profits they might eventually realize by selling advertising time in the new medium.

Commercial television broadcasting began in a limited way in 1941 but was temporarily abandoned at the start of World War II. Plans to launch the new media technology in the United States were resumed following the end of hostilities in 1945. Less than a year later, television broadcasting in America began (Barnouw, 1975, pp. 72, 92, 100).

Only 6,000 television sets were sold to Americans in 1946. The following year that number jumped to 179,000 (Sterling & Haight, 1978, p. 360). As the FCC began licensing television stations to operate, four networks emerged to provide programing: NBC, CBS, DuMont (owned by Alan B. DuMont, an inventor and appliance manufacturer), and ABC. Almost all of the programing originated from New York City, Chicago, or Los Angeles. In 1955 the struggling DuMont network collapsed and ABC captured most of its affiliated stations. For the next thirty years, the three remaining companies dominated the network television power structure (DeLuca, 1980, p. 135).

1948: TELEVISION BECOMES A PRACTICAL REALITY

In 1948, generally regarded as the year when commercial broadcast television emerged as a major mass medium in the United States, only seventeen stations were broadcasting. Within a year there were fifty-one. To a significant extent, the rapid growth of the network television industry is attributable to the fact that it was built on the existing and prosperous framework of network radio. Network radio affiliates applied for and usually won permission from the FCC to build local television stations. As soon as they were operating, these local stations quickly became affiliated with the new television networks.

Each station already had a sales organization, advertisers and their advertising agencies, and program providers, who were eager to do business in the new medium. Radio stars—such as Arthur Godfrey, Ted Mack, and Milton Berle—made swift and successful transitions from network radio to network television, building enormous audiences and stimulating a powerful demand for television sets among American consumers. In the beginning, advertising spots were crudely executed; but the agencies soon learned how to maximize television's selling potential, allowing marketers to demonstrate their products dramatically in ways that had never before been possible through a mass medium. As the new medium's power to communicate advertisers' messages effectively was understood, the advertising industry embraced network television with an enduring passion (Heighton & Cunningham, 1976, pp. 25, 26).

Historian Daniel J. Boorstin (Adler, 1981) observed, "Of all the wonders of TV, none is more remarkable than the speed with which it came." Adler noted that "the printing press took five centuries to achieve its full impact. Television required less than a generation" (p. xi).

By 1950, network radio was dying and network television was burgeoning. Network television achieved full national capability in

September 1951, when a new coast-to-coast coaxial cable allowed ninety-four television stations to carry simultaneously an address by President Harry S. Truman. This broadcast was received by 95 percent of the country's television sets, with an audience estimated at about 1 million. A year later, the FCC lifted the "freeze" it had ordered in 1948 on the expansion of television stations, allowing the network affiliate system to accelerate at an even faster pace (Sterling & Kittross, 1978, pp. 260–67). (Table 3.2 shows the number of television stations in the United States 1947–1987).

NETWORK TELEVISION REPLACES RADIO AS KEY MEDIUM

Television penetration of U.S. households grew from less than 10 percent in 1950 to 40 percent by 1953. From 1955 to 1965, the number of American homes with at least one television set grew from 66 percent to more than 90 percent. During that period, it was not unusual for a popular network show to earn a rating in the 1950s, which means that 50 percent of all possible television homes in the United States were tuned to that show. A rating of that magnitude is almost impossible to attain in the current fragmented media environment. *I Love Lucy*, a particularly popular weekly show of that period, earned an average 60 rating during the 1953–1954 season, according to A. C. Nielsen. The next five most popular shows earned average ratings between 50 and 58.

An especially significant year in television history was 1953, when television's advertising volume finally equalled that of radio. In 1952, television advertising revenue had been one-third less than that of radio. Since 1954, television's advertising earnings have outstripped radio's by increasingly substantial amounts ("A Broadcast History," 1983).

THE TV NETWORKS BEGIN TO USE VIDEOTAPE IN 1956

The CBS Television Network was the first to use the Ampex system to broadcast from videotape, presenting *Douglas Edwards and the News* in 1956 (Schubin, 1986, p. 50). The system was next used by CBS early in 1957 for *Arthur Godfrey's Talent Scouts*. The Ampex videotape recorder dominated the professional videotape-recording field until its technology was embraced, and ultimately improved upon, by competitive forces in the marketplace.

The successful adoption of the previously described Ampex system brought about more than technological change. Before video recording became standard, television network executives had assumed that the only acceptable way to satisfy their viewers was with live

Table 3.2
Number of Network–Affiliated Television Stations, 1947–1987

Year	Total Commercial Stations	Total Network Affiliates n	%
1947	12	4	33
1948	6	16	100
1949	51	50	98
1950	98	96	98
1951	107	107	100
1952	107	108	100
1953	126	125	99
1954	354	317	90
1955	411	374	91
1956	441	421	95
1957	471	445	94
1958	495	469	95
1959	510	485	95
1960	515	496	96
1961	527	503	95
1962	541	508	94
1963	557	514	92
1964	564	526	93
1965	569	516	91
1966	585	532	91
1967	610	537	88
1968	635	547	86
1969	662	557	84
1970	677	568	84
1971	682	593	87
1972	693	599	86
1973	697	604	87
1974	697	611	88
1975	706	617	87
1976	701	613	87
1977	711	612	86
1978	716	616	86
1979	724	623	86
1980	734	615	84
1981	756	620	82
1982	777	621	80
1983	813	N/A	N/A
1984	841	N/A	N/A
1985	883	N/A	N/A
1986	924	N/A	N/A
1987	971	N/A	N/A

Sources: To 1982, C.H. Sterling, *Electronic media: A guide to trends in broadcasting and new technologies 1920–1983*, New York: Praeger (1984), p. 24. Reprinted with permission of Praeger. From 1983 to 1987, *Trends in television*, Television Bureau of Advertising (TvB), (June 1987), p. 11. Reprinted with permission of Television Bureau of Advertising.

programing. With the exception of motion pictures originally produced for theatrical release (a television mainstay from the medium's inception), virtually everything produced especially for television was done "live." News event, sports and dramatic and variety shows were seen by television audiences as they occurred.

Because of the three-hour time difference between the U.S. east and west coasts and the fact that almost every significant program originated in New York City, this practice had a serious impact on viewership levels. For example, a television network news program produced at 7 P.M. in New York was simultaneously broadcast at 4 P.M. in Los Angeles, thus eliminating large numbers of potential viewers who were still at work. Additionally, daylight-savings time, which was not put into effect in all U.S. localities, caused scheduling confusion. Kinescope recordings of news shows proved to be completely undesirable to audiences and were never used seriously by the three networks for other than archival storage.

Consequently, the Ampex videotape system was swiftly adopted by broadcasters since it allowed the television networks to air the same show at the same "clock time" throughout the country ("Birth of a new Era," 1956). Nayak and Ketteringham (1986, p. 25) noted that live television began to decline as a unique communication medium on the day the Ampex engineers finished work on the first videotape recorder.

Before the Ampex system was in general use, television networks functioned in a pure video version of what Ong (1982, p. 74) described as an "oral culture." Previously, both the storyteller and those listening had to be present when the story was told. As the storytellers (or television producers) began to videotape their shows for later broadcast, the sense of intimacy between storyteller and audience began to change. Dramatic sequences in which actors forgot lines or sneezed after being "shot dead" were no longer seen. They were replaced by flawless productions, the result of endless videotaped retakes until perfection was achieved. The tension, spontaneity, and heightened sense of awareness that permeate any live performance were lost as audiences began to accept the new prerecorded reality. This early exposure to taped television may have started preparing viewers for the time when they would take videotaping into their own hands and manipulate the shows—fast-forwarding them through scenes lacking significant actions or deleting commercials—to please themselves.

While the term "time-shifting" was not introduced until years later, it would seem that Bing Crosby's determination to be on the golf course while his audience listened to or watched him perform was the impetus that ultimately freed the public from the constraints of watching programs only at the times at which they were broadcast.

Or, as Brown (1979, p. 45) observed, taping liberated the consumer from the agendas set by networks and local stations and let the listener or viewer become the programer.

While Ampex consolidated its position as the dominant entity in professional videotape recording, other companies in the United States and overseas began to explore the potential of this technology for home use.

THE RELATIONSHIP OF ADVERTISERS AND THE NETWORKS

From the early 1950s until the early 1960s, advertisers and their advertising agencies profoundly influenced the form and content of network television in the United States. During this period, often called the "Golden Age of Television," a group of extraordinarily talented writers, directors, and performers produced a series of dramatic and comedy shows retrospectively regarded as the most outstanding in the medium's history. In general, each program was sponsored by a single advertiser, which took great pride in its associa- tion with the show and frequently influenced its creative direction. This pattern was a holdover from network radio, for which national advertisers and their agencies created, supervised, and controlled most of the programing on the air. In the heyday of network radio and the early years of network television, a network was no more than what Brown (1971) described as "a conveyance" (p. 65) that distributed the sponsors' programs to the public over the affiliated stations' airwaves.

As the cost of advertising on network television escalated, decreas- ing numbers of advertisers were able to afford sponsorship of an entire program. Additionally, Barnouw (1978, p. 55) noted that a scandal in- volving a wholly sponsored quiz show influenced the networks to discourage single advertisers from continuing to control the programing content of individual shows or series. Led by ABC, the net- works began selling one-minute sponsorships on a number of programs at various times of the day and on different days of the week. This change in the method of sponsorship was called "scatter participation" (Tuchman, 1974, p. 100). It initiated a trend that effectively shifted con- trol of programing and program content from the advertisers and their agencies to the networks. To a large extent, the networks have retained control of these aspects of their operations ever since.

NETWORK TELEVISION FROM 1964 TO 1975

By 1964, out of a total of 56 million U.S. households, more than 92 percent—almost 52 million of U.S. homes—owned at least one television set. An average of five hours and twenty-fives minutes per television household was spent on television viewing each day and the annual total network share of the U.S. television audience during prime time was 92 percent (Television Bureau of Advertising, 1987d).

While network television sales figures did not match the double— and even triple—digit increases that characterized the medium's growth from 1948 to 1956, 1964 was a year in which the three television networks increased their combined revenues by $107 million to $1.1 billion, a gain of more than 9 percent over 1963's performance (Television Bureau of Advertising, 1987b). This growth was part of the continuing profit pattern that had been developing since the inception of network television broadcasting in the United States.

Many of the issues that would later confound the networks were already beginning to surface. One was the rising cost of producing programing. Another was the increase in complaints by advertisers about commercial clutter (the numerous commercial interruptions in television programs). While the sixty-second commercial was still the dominant advertising format on network television, the thirty-second commercial was beginning to replace it. An emerging third issue was the problem of accommodating the technical shift from black-and-white to color programing and broadcasting ("1964 Record," 1965).

Extensive television coverage of national events in the early 1960s caused Americans to start considering network television their primary source of immediate information. These included the 1963 saturation television coverage surrounding the assassination of President John F. Kennedy on November 22 and, two days later, the killing of his alleged assassin on live network television. Regular network television news coverage was dramatically expanded as all three networks increased their evening news shows from fifteen minutes to the half-hour format that presently prevails.

In the area of entertainment, top-rated network series included *Bonanza, The Beverly Hillbillies, Gilligan's Island,* and *Peyton Place,* long-running shows that are still seen in syndication on independent nonnetwork-affiliated stations (Goldstein & Goldstein, 1983, pp. 187–88, 195–96).

In the late 1960s, network television began to experience further changes. There were 1.6 million U.S. households with color television sets, representing 3.1 percent of all television homes in 1964. Five years later, there were 18.7 million color television households in the country. Thirty-two percent of all U.S. households had a color television set. Color became the dominant mode for both television programing and the production of commercials. Additionally, more

American households began to have multiple television sets, with 30.9 percent of all homes owning more than one television set by 1969 (Television Bureau of Advertising, 1987b). Multiple set ownership inevitably produced greater opportunities for individual viewing experiences within the home. Since A. C. Nielsen Co. only monitored the viewing of a single television set in the home, this change created new problems affecting ratings measurement. Further, commercial interruptions of network programing were proliferating, causing advertisers and their agencies to become increasingly concerned about the effects of "clutter" on network audiences. Since the availability of desirable time slots for commercials could not be expanded, the networks encouraged the use of thirty-second commercials to the point at which sixty-second spots virtually ceased to be used. Ten-second commercials were also being utilized more frequently by affiliated stations for two reasons: to maximize their stations' revenue during local commercial breaks and to encourage local advertisers, with smaller budgets, to employ the television medium ("For Radio—TV," 1966).

Concerned industry observers cited the growing number of alternative broadcast media, especially independent television stations, as an important reason why advertising's cost was going up at the same time as its effectiveness was decreasing. The larger number of independent television stations caused already splintering audiences to become even more fragmented.

The television networks were also developing a greater awareness and concern regarding the effects of Community Antenna Television (CATV) as increasing numbers of American homes were hooked up to cable systems. This proliferation of media was beginning to make mass audiences, previously easily reachable by advertisers on network television, less accessible and more expensive to reach. Another commonly expressed worry was network television's trend toward clustering commercials into predictably spaced "pods," which increased a viewer's tendency to ignore the commercials during extended program interruptions.

In 1968 the networks' combined advertising revenues exceeded $1.5 billion. After reaching its peak of 93 percent in 1966, the annual total network television prime-time share of the U.S. television audience in 1968 was 91 percent and starting downward, although the average time spent watching television had increased by twenty-one minutes daily to five hours and forty-six minutes per household. In 1968 audiences also witnessed the unruly Democratic convention in Chicago and the street battles between anti-war demonstrators and the police. During that season, *60 Minutes* premiered on CBS, beginning a run that continues today. By the end of 1968, an estimated 14 million U.S.

homes were equipped with color television, representing approximately 30 percent of total television sets ("Television: No Great Upswing," 1968), and there were 57.5 million television households in the United States ("ARB Nationwide," 1969).

An estimated 125 million Americans—reportedly the largest single television audience in the history of the medium to that time—were watching network television on July 20, 1969, as astronauts Neil Armstrong and Edwin E. Aldrin, Jr., walked on the moon. It was during the late 1960s (Brown, 1979, p. 73) that advertisers became dissatisfied with simply reaching the greatest number of television viewers of the shows they were sponsoring. The advertising industry consensus agreed some viewers were more worth reaching than others. Advertisers considered American viewers desirable in this order: first, ages 18–34 (especially women); next, ages 18–49; and finally, viewers under age 18 or over age 49. Since the advertisers' research indicated the most commercially viable audiences were regular moviegoers who enjoyed seeing sex and violence depicted, the networks began developing shows that contained increasingly permissive scenes showing far more sex and violence than had earlier been permitted on network television. As the networks began to produce shows appealing to smaller and more economically desirable audience segments, shows that appealed to larger but older audiences—such as the still popular *Bonanza*—were canceled. Series primarily appealing to children or viewers in rural areas were also replaced (Reel, 1979, pp. 8–9). As these programing changes occurred, the networks became the object of a rising tide of Congressional concern that ultimately caused ABC, CBS, and NBC to reduce the amount of violence portrayed in children's and prime-time program periods. After 1970, Congress ordered the cigarette industry to stop advertising its products on all forms of broadcast media (Barnouw, 1978, p. 87). This decision left the television networks with 3,829 minutes of commercial time, previously bought by the cigarette companies for approximately $250 million annually, to be filled by other advertisers ("Agnew's Blast," 1969).

By 1970, more than 95 percent of all U.S. homes had a black-and-white television set, 40 percent had a color set, and Americans were watching the medium for increasingly longer periods each day. According to the Television Bureau of Advertising, average daily viewing in U.S. television households gradually climbed from five hours and fifty minutes in 1969 to six hours and twelve minutes in 1972 (Television Bureau of Advertising, 1987d). The year 1972 included the network debuts of *Marcus Welby, M.D.*, *The Brady Bunch* and *Room 222*; and the end of NBC's long-running *Huntley-Brinkley Report*, an evening news show (Goldstein & Goldstein, 1983, pp. 233–34, 241–42).

Additionally, in 1972 more than 60 percent of all television households were equipped with at least one color set.

As early as 1971, a CBS Television research report predicted video-cassette recorder viewing would not take place at the expense of regular television viewing (Bogart, 1972, p. xxxi). It was during this period—before alternative electronic media technologies began to have a significant impact on American television viewing habits—that DeLuca (1980) observed the networks "reached the pinnacle of their success" (p. 143).

The early 1970s also saw the introduction of shows reflecting the climate of social protest that was happening in the United States. Themes and life-styles that were previously avoided because of the networks' fear of criticism were now being dramatized. Stories involving drug abuse, sexually related diseases, and mental illness were presented for the first time in prime-time network shows. Bill Cosby and Flip Wilson, the first black performers to break the de facto color barrier, starred in their own series. Such major hits as *The Odd Couple* and *The Mary Tyler Moore Show* also made their debuts. However, *All in the Family* was the show that did more than any other to introduce subjects previously considered taboo by the networks. Using comedy, this show presented stories dealing with racial and religious prejudice, abortion, and homosexuality. It was the forerunner of the scores of equally outspoken shows that followed and demonstrated to network executives and advertisers that American network television viewers were prepared to accept far more realistic and sensitive issues as the subjects of prime-time programs (Goldstein & Goldstein, 1983, pp. 241–42, 247–48).

In 1971 the FCC imposed the Prime Time Access Rule (PTAR) on the networks, requiring them to surrender the first half-hour of the three and one-half hours of prime-time scheduling they controlled each evening to their affiliated stations for local programing. The primary purpose of this rule was to encourage greater diversity of programing sources, particularly among affiliated stations. However, this time period became filled to a great extent by syndicated game shows produced in Los Angeles (Head & Sterling, 1972, p. 339). According to Back (1979), "The FCC had accomplished its aim of greater program diversity in the marketplace and had created more sources of programs for television stations" (p. ii). He also noted that PTAR "altered the structure of prime time and the relationship of groups within the commercial television industry." One effect of the change accomplished by the PTAR, he said, was a decline in network-affiliated stations' audiences in the five-year period following the ruling's introduction.

Color television was in 55 percent of all American homes by 1973 and viewers were spending more time watching television: a household average of six hours and fifteen minutes a day. After dipping to an annual three-network prime-time share of 88 percent in 1971, the networks' combined share returned to 92 percent by 1973. During this period, police dramas—such as *Kojak, Starsky and Hutch,* and *Police Story*—were establishing themselves and situation comedies—such as *Maude, Happy Days, The Jeffersons* and *Chico and the Man*—began what became extended runs. Prime-time programing became more offbeat, with such shows as *Cannon* and *Colombo* featuring unglamorous characters who looked and behaved increasingly like their viewers. The Korean war series *M*A*S*H* was also launched during this period, beginning an eleven-year prime-time network run. This show's final episode generated the highest rating for a series episode in the history of television. The Watergate hearings also dominated the consciousness of the nation's viewers during this time. The networks provided 300 hours of rotating coverage and audience research indicated that 85 percent of all television homes were tuned to at least part of one day's proceedings. This massive television coverage and the network reporting that followed the hearings culminated on August 8, 1974, when President Richard M. Nixon went on live network television to announce his resignation (Goldstein & Goldstein, 1983, pp. 271–72, 278–79).

In 1975 97 percent of all U.S. households owned a television set; 68 percent owned color sets. During that year all three television networks committed themselves to a policy wherein the first hour of network prime time was considered a "family hour" and contained programs with less sex and violence than those appearing later in the evening. The networks' joint decision was influenced by then FCC Chairman Richard C. Wiley, who reportedly coerced the networks' managements into the agreement. Although a federal court judge subsequently found Wiley's actions unconstitutional, the National Association of Broadcasters incorporated the "Family Viewing Time" concept into its television code (Brown 1977, p. 147). This network programing pattern has been largely maintained to date.

NETWORK TELEVISION PROGRAMING PATTERNS: 1975 TO THE PRESENT

The mid-1970s have come to be regarded as the broadcast television networks' apogee. The three networks were riding high, making record profits and capturing the largest combined audiences they were ever to have. As described in a previous chapter, it was also the period when the videocassette recorder was introduced to consumer markets in the United States. There is no indication the networks' senior executives had any realistic appreciation at that time about the ways in which the VCR would ultimately impact on their industry.

When Sony launched its U.S. marketing program for the Betamax videocassette recorder in the fall of 1975, the videocassette recorder was not regarded as a new media technology of threatening significance to the three broadcast networks. *Television Digest's* Editorial Director David Lachenbruch (personal communication, October 19, 1987) recalled he interviewed the programing heads of the ABC, CBS, and NBC Television Networks shortly after Sony announced the introduction of the Betamax videocassette recorder in the United States. He said none of them expressed the least apprehension about the effect of the new product on the business of broadcast television, considering the Betamax to be just another consumer appliance, "like a toaster."

TV Guide's New York Bureau Chief Neil Hickey (personal communication, January 19, 1988) suggested one reason why the network executives (and most other people in the mass media industry) did not recognize the videocassette recorder's possible impact was there was so much attention being paid to the market potential of video disc technology at the time, with such companies as RCA investing several hundred million dollars in development and promotion to support the video disc as the dominant new U.S. home entertainment system. Hickey (1982) noted that by the time these companies launched their competing versions of the video disc in the U.S. consumer mass market, the videocassette recorder had already established itself as a popular consumer product, "with enthusiastic partisans who prefer its features to those of the disc" (p. 14). NBC's former head of planning and research Hugh M. Beville (personal communication, January 27, 1988) said he believed the television networks largely ignored the videocassette recorder in the home because "they are generally not very perceptive about the future. . . . It's a general attitude [network management has] about new things."

Sony began to promote its new product aggressively in February 1976. The advertising prepared by Sony's advertising agency, Doyle Dane Bernbach, specifically proposed that the primary use for the Betamax was as a "video time-shift machine" for the recording and playback of broadcast programs ("First Home VTR Deck," 1976, p. 9). Lyons (1976) described Sony Chairman Akio Morita's philosophy, upon which the advertising campaign was based, as being, "Any time is prime time" (p. 210). By the end of 1976, 55,000 videocassette recorders had been sold to U.S. dealers ("Color TV Analogy" 1984). There were almost 70 million television households in the United States, representing 97.4 percent of all U.S. homes, and American viewers were spending an average of six hours and eighteen minutes per household every day watching television (Television Bureau of Advertising, 1987b).

All three networks participated in the coverage of the nation's day-long 200th birthday party on July 4, 1976. The highest rated dramatic show in the history of network television, *Roots*, was broadcast over eight consecutive nights. Former President Richard M. Nixon was interviewed in four ninety-minute telecasts shown over an ad hoc special network of 185 stations. It proved to be the highest rated news/interview show in history. In 1976, the movie classic, *Gone with the Wind*, was shown on television for the first time and scored the highest rating for a movie in television history (Goldstein & Goldstein, 1983, pp. 301–2).

It was during the 1975–1976 television season that the three major networks achieved a total prime-time share of 93 percent of the U.S. television audience, a position of dominance equalled only once before —in 1966—and unlikely ever to be repeated. Each network was affiliated with more than 200 commercial stations, the same number that prevails today (Head & Sterling, 1987, p. 199). However, in the years that followed, the growing popularity of the home videocassette recorder, combined with the proliferation of cable television—then in only 12.6 percent of America's television households; and the increase of independent commercial broadcast television stations (706 were operating at that time in the United States) began inexorably to erode the audience base of the networks. This downward trend has not been arrested to date.

After years of being the least successful television network, ABC took a dominant position in the prime-time ratings battle in 1977, presenting seven of the season's top ten rated prime-time shows. That year it also launched *The Love Boat* and *Fantasy Island*, both of which became long-term successes featuring different guest stars in each week's episodes. During that season, CBS premiered the dramatic series *Dallas*, a prime-time soap opera in the tradition of the 1960s ABC success, *Peyton Place*. *Dallas* spawned a succession of equally celebrated imitators, reestablishing the genre as a popular network prime-time series format (Goldstein & Goldstein, 1983, pp. 315–16). But the total network prime-time share had begun to slip from its peak of 93 percent to 92 percent ("A. C. Nielsen," 1987). While videocassette recorder sales to dealers had more than doubled over the previous year to 160,000 ("Color TV Analogy," 1984), network television executives continued to remain unconcerned about the effect of the videocassette recorder. Harry Smith, CBS corporate planning vice president, said, "We're not preoccupied with the impact of the VCR." NBC planning vice president Alfred Ordover said, "Even at [a retail cost of] $700–800 . . . effective fractionalization of the broadcast market is minor. It won't have a tremendous effect one way or the other." *Television Digest* ("Networks Unconcerned," 1977, p. 8) quoted another senior network executive, without identifying him, as saying, "Videocassettes are likely to be limited to hobbyist use, like the audio cassette in relation to radio. I doubt we could measure the impact negatively or positively within a ten year horizon." A leading broadcasting trade publication ("VTR's: Breaking and Entering the Home Market," 1977, p. 28) noted market studies had shown "that a large percentage of buyers [of videocassette recorders] are people with odd-hour jobs, such as nurses, janitors, and airline pilots." It suggested, however, that another reason for the product's sales was "just about to anyone, especially in this American age of individualism, the ability to take control of your television set is an attractive proposition." A former NBC executive, Hugh Beville, observed, "This is the first time programing is becoming unhinged from its time period. This may be more significant than pay television or cable. When there are 2-5 million [VCRS] out there, the effect on television programing will be tremendous" ("Networks Unconcerned," 1977, p. 8).

In 1978, as the alternative viewing options available to network television viewers increased, the networks contributed to the breakup of stable viewing patterns by accelerating the rate of programing changes. Preoccupied with challenging one another for dominance in the battle for ratings, the networks continued to ignore the explosive growth in U.S. videocassette recorder sales to dealers, which had doubled again over the previous year to 401,900 ("Color TV Analogy," 1984); the increasing encroachment of satellite-delivered cable television programing; and the rising number of nonnetwork-affiliated commercial television stations competing for viewers in local U.S. markets. While the total U.S. population, the percentage of households with television, and the average number of daily hours spent viewing television continued to grow (Television Bureau of Advertising, 1987b), the networks' share of the total prime-time audience was eroded again—to 91 percent—in 1978 ("A. C. Nielsen," 1987).

Throughout most of the season that began in 1979, network television news programing was dominated by the ongoing story about the seizure of the U.S. Embassy and more than sixty U.S. hostages in Iran. Generally, the networks began to give greater emphasis to news during prime time as they were confronted by the newly launched Cable News Network (CNN), which provided news to cable television systems twenty-four hours daily. Cable was in more than 18 percent of all U.S. television households and both advertiser-supported and pay cable networks were proliferating (Television Bureau of Advertising, 1987a). The annual total network prime-time share of the television audience continued to diminish—to 90 percent ("A. C. Nielsen," 1987)—and A. C. Nielsen Company reported that there were now 475,000 videocassette recorders in U.S. households, representing one half of 1 percent of total television households (Television Bureau of Advertising, 1987b). Commenting on the threat that new electronic media technologies posed to the traditional network television system, then NBC president Fred Silverman told the National Academy of Television Arts and Sciences in Los Angeles that "it will be years, if ever, before other technologies come close to delivering the kind of audience that would justify those [production] costs. Only the national distribution which the networks have enables us to do that." ("NBC on Technology," 1979, p. 5). During his talk, Mr. Silverman also disparaged program suppliers' dreams of "selling your programs directly to fourth networks, superstations, cable outlets, magnetized bubblegum wrappers and forty-eight other technologies" (p. 5).

An Arbitron study of videocassette recorder owners released in 1979 revealed that 75 percent of those surveyed said they bought the machines for time-shift purposes. Only 11 percent of those in the study deleted commercials while viewing previously taped shows. The study concluded commercial deletion was "unlikely to become a problem unless a system is developed to delete commercials automatically" ("How People Use VCRs," 1979, p. 11).

Several dour predictions of network television's future were offered during 1979. Sylvester "Pat" Weaver, former NBC president, prophesied that "the networks are going to lose at least one half of their audience" and that their future strength would be dependent on live programing ("Cable & Ad Agencies," 1979, p. 3). Harold Vogel, a Merrill-Lynch financial analyst, said, "Technological termites are eating at the foundation [of broadcasting]. Fragmentation of the television audience will mimic what happened in national magazines in the last twenty-five years" ("Futurists Describe 80s," 1979, p. 5). Mr. Vogel was referring to the demise of *Life, Look*, and *The Saturday Evening Post*, general interest publications that went out of business in the early 1960s at the height of their circulation growth.

In April 1979 Sony introduced a new feature for the Betamax that was quickly imitated by its VHS competitors because of its enormous popularity. It was called the Betascan. This device allowed owners of videocassette recorders to retain the video picture on the screen while operating in the fast-forward and rewind modes. The visible fast-forward feature was immediately embraced by the American public as a means to speed through the commercials which interrupted network television programs ("Sony 1980," 1979). David Lachenbruch stated that:

> this was unquestionably the biggest landmark improvement
> in the history of the videocassette recorder. Before visible fast-
> forward, there was no way anybody could zip through the

commercials, because you'd have to guess where they ended and the program you were watching began. But this feature gave you the opportunity of seeing exactly where the commercials ended. (personal communication, October 19, 1987)

The 1980 network prime-time television season got off to a late start as the unions representing actors waged a lengthy strike to gain a share of the profits earned from the sale of film and series rights distributed to pay television networks and from prerecorded videocassettes. As a result, the season, which normally begins in September, was delayed until November. While fewer new shows were introduced that year, several series began enduring runs. These included *Hill Street Blues, Magnum P.I.,* and *Dynasty.* It was also the year in which Walter Cronkite retired as the anchorman of *The CBS Evening News* after nineteen years, to be replaced by Dan Rather. The number of households with videocassette recorders more than doubled to 840,000, representing 1.1 percent of all American television homes in 1980 (Television Bureau of Advertising, 1987b), and the annual total network prime-time share of the U.S. television audience dropped two percentage points in that year to eighty-eight percent ("A. C. Nielsen," 1987).

This increased rate of erosion was coincidental with the start of the rapid acquisition rate of videocassette recorders by Americans. Arnie Semsky (personal communication, February 17, 1988), executive vice president in charge of media and programing at BBDO, Worldwide, recalled network executives first began reacting to the impact of the videocassette recorder when they discovered that college students and people working in offices during the day were time-shifting daytime "soaps" for later viewing. In 1980 a study of the use of the videocassette recorder in television households—sponsored by the National Association of Broadcasters (NAB)—revealed almost 80 percent of the television programs taped and replayed were originally broadcast on network-affiliated stations. Only 4 percent of all playbacks were recorded from cable and pay television channels combined. Time-shifting was found to be the primary use of videocassette recorders, and motion pictures, situation comedies, and soap operas were the principal videotaped categories (National Association of Broadcasters, 1980). During that year, Gene Secunda, a senior vice president of J. Walter Thompson Co., told the annual convention of the American Advertising Federation that one of the three major television networks would be driven to focus its energies exclusively on cable programing in the "not-too-distant future" ("Big Network Expected to Focus on Cable TV," 1980, p. 15).

The 1981 network television season was delayed by a writer's strike over the issue of revenues earned from the new video technologies.

Numerous series were canceled and new shows were launched as the networks battled each other to gain control over the diminishing network television prime-time audience. Network executives were also reacting to increasing complaints from organized groups protesting for a reduction in the amount of sex and violence being depicted in prime-time programs. Several highly rated shows, including *Charlie's Angels* and *Vega$*, were the object of much protest and were cancelled during the season (Goldstein & Goldstein, 1983, pp. 365–66). There were now almost one and one-half million videocassette recorders in American homes, representing 1.8 percent of all television households (Television Bureau of Advertising, 1987b). The number of commercial broadcast television stations continued to grow (offering increasing competition for network-affiliated stations throughout the United States); cable television penetration of U.S. households increased to more than 22 percent (Television Bureau of Advertising, 1987a); and the rate of total network prime-time share erosion dropped five points to 83 percent, representing the greatest loss of audience since A. C. Nielsen began measuring this trend ("A. C. Nielsen," 1987).

By 1982, hour-long prime-time dramas based on the daytime soap opera format were becoming a dominant factor on network television. *Dynasty, Falcon Crest,* and *Knot's Landing* had become established series with high ratings. Other types of series—such as *Hill Street Blues* and *Cheers*—were also utilizing the technique of continuing stories (Brooks & Marsh, 1985, p. xx). Total prime-time network share of the television audience dropped another three points from the previous year to 80 percent ("A. C. Nielsen," 1987). Cable was in almost 30 percent of all U.S. television households and more than 3 percent of those homes owned a videocassette recorder (Television Bureau of Advertising, 1987b).

By 1983, there were 13 million more television households in the United States than there had been in 1975, when Sony introduced the Betamax videocassette recorder. (See Table 3.3 for total number of television households 1950–1987.) The average time spent watching television in each home was now seven hours and two minutes, almost an hour more than in 1975. Cable television was in one of every three U.S. television households and videocassette recorders were being used in more than 5 percent of those homes. In 1983 there were 813 commercial television stations in America, 107 more than in 1975 (Television Bureau of Advertising, 1987b). While series based on fantasy continued to be popular, new series examining the lighter side of people's actual lives—such as *Real People, That's Incredible* and *Ripley's Believe It or Not*—had become staples of the networks' prime-time schedules (Brooks & Marsh, 1985, p. xx). The three networks'

Table 3.3
Total Number of Television Households, 1950–1987

	Total U.S. Households (000)	TV Households (000)	% with TV
1950	43,000	3,880	9.0
1951	43,890	10,320	23.5
1952	44,760	15,300	34.2
1953	45,640	20,400	44.7
1954	46,660	26,000	55.7
1955	47,620	30,700	64.5
1956	48,600	34,900	71.8
1957	49,500	38,900	78.6
1958	50,370	41,920	83.2
1959	51,150	43,950	85.9
1960	52,500	45,750	87.1
1961	53,170	47,200	88.8
1962	54,300	48,855	90.0
1963	55,100	50,300	91.3
1964	55,900	51,600	92.3
1965	56,900	52,700	92.6
1966	57,900	53,850	93.0
1967	58,900	55,130	93.6
1968	59,900	56,670	94.6
1969	61,300	58,250	95.0
1970	61,410	58,500	95.3
1971	62,910	60,100	95.5
1972	64,850	62,100	95.8
1973	67,210	64,800	96.4
1974	68,310	66,200	96.9
1975	70,520	68,500	97.1
1976	71,460	69,600	97.4
1977	73,100	71,200	97.4
1978	74,700	72,900	97.6
1979	76,240	74,500	97.7
1980	77,900	76,300	97.9
1981	81,480	79,900	98.1
1982	83,120	81,500	98.1
1983	84,940	83,300	98.1
1984	85,430	83,800	98.1
1985	86,530	84,900	98.1
1987	87,590	85,900	98.1
1987	89,130	87,400	98.1

Source: Trends in television, Television Bureau of Advertising (TvB), (June 1987), p. 3. Reprinted with permission of Television Bureau of Advertising.

prime-time share of the television audience fell four additional points from 1982 to 76 percent ("A. C. Nielsen," 1987). Videocassette recorders were still in only a limited number of U.S. homes, but debate about their potential impact on network viewing and television commercials was becoming pronounced. A study sponsored by the Motion Picture Association of America reported 68 percent of videocassette recorder owners were deleting commercials while replaying programs recorded from commercial television. It also stated three out of every five people who recorded programs skipped over commercials during playback. The Association's study further found that 93 percent of videocassette recording resulted in time-shifting, which threatened commercial television "by interfering with viewing of time-sensitive advertising and precluding advertisers from targeting audiences" ("VCR Users," 1983).

In 1984, A. C. Nielsen published its major study of the effects of the videocassette recorder on television viewing. It revealed 36 percent of the study's respondents said they used the "stop" or "pause" feature of the unit to delete commercials in television shows they were both recording and watching. Thirty-six percent said they did so usually (73 percent or more of the time), 10 percent said frequently (50 to 74 percent of the time) and 10 percent said occasionally (15 to 49 percent), 17 percent said seldom (less than 25 percent), 14 percent said never, and 13 percent said they did not view while recording.

In response to a question concerning frequency of use of the "speed-search" or "fast-forward" capability of the machine in order to skip over commercials when playing back a television show recorded with them, 49 percent said that they skipped usually, 10 percent said frequently, 11 percent said occasionally, 14 percent said seldom, and 16 percent said never ("Getting a Fix," 1984).

Network spokespeople and others associated with the broadcasting business argued that the impact of the videocassette recorder on television viewing and the commercial avoidance issue was overstated by the Nielsen report. Tony Hoffman, director of corporate finance for Craline & Company, observed "people are paying more attention to the video than they would if they had no control over it. I would submit that you [the viewers watching videotaped television pro-. grams] are actually getting better retention." David Poltrack, then vice president of research at CBS, said, "It would appear that the overall level of network viewing in a household will be increased by VCR ownership" ("The Competition," 1984, p. 53).

In 1984 a new series starring Bill Cosby, called *The Cosby Show*, premiered; it subsequently became one of the highest rated comedy series on network television. That season, a lavishly produced police drama called *Miami Vice* also premiered, setting the pattern for the entry of other hour-long prime-time series comprised of single episodes costing more than $1 million each. Cable was in more than 39 percent of all U.S. television households and videocassette recorders were in one of every ten of those homes (Television Bureau of Advertising, 1987b). Network television's total prime-time share of the U.S. audience had stopped eroding for the first time since 1975, holding at 76 percent ("A. C. Nielsen," 1987).

By 1985, there were 17.7 million U.S. homes in which there was at least one videocassette recorder, an increase of more than 10 percent over the previous year to 20.8 percent of all households. Cable was in 42.8 percent of all U.S. television homes. While each television network continued to have approximately 200 affiliated stations, the number of nonaffiliated stations increased. In 1985 there were 883 commercial television stations in the U.S., 25 percent more than there had been in 1975. The average daily time spent viewing television in each home had reached a record high of seven hours and ten minutes (Television Bureau of Advertising, 1987b). New data from A. C. Nielsen, which was monitoring the effect of videocassette recorder usage on television on a weekly basis, revealed many top-rated network programs were being extensively videotaped without being played back ("New Nielsen VCR Data," 1985). This issue was somewhat clouded by the publication of other studies, sponsored by the broadcasting industry, which stated that almost all programs taped for later viewing are viewed and many are viewed more than once ("Home Tape Study Cues Web Grins," 1985). As a result of this confusion, various elements of the mass media and marketing communications industries began to demand more reliable and consistent standards of measurement of the effect that videocassette recording was having on television viewing patterns.

During the 1985–1986 season, a new situation comedy series called *Golden Girls* was introduced and became a highly rated hit. The show, featuring four mature women, represented the first significant effort any network had made to appeal to older prime-time television viewers since the late 1960s (BBDO, 1986). This programing trend reflected an awareness that the median age of the U.S. population, which had lowered during the ten years following the 1960 census (1960–29.4 years; 1970–27.9 years) had been steadily aging since the 1970 census to the point at which the median age of the United States had become 31.5 years by 1985. Fifty-six percent of total income and expenditures was accounted for by Americans age forty-five or older (Bureau of the Census, 1987, pp. 14, 428).

By the end of 1986, 36 percent of all U.S. television households had at least one videocassette recorder and cable penetration had increased to more than 45 percent of those homes. There were 924 commercial television stations in the country (Television Bureau of Advertising, 1987b). Following the success of *The Cosby Show* and *Golden Girls*, situation comedies based on outspoken characters and the depiction of unusual personal problems became increasingly popular. The action/adventure/mystery series formats, which had been mainstays of the networks for many years, were losing popularity, as were such extravagantly produced hour-long prime-time soap operas as *Dallas*. As owners of videocassette recorders relied increasingly on neighborhood video rental stores for their Hollywood movie entertainment, the networks substituted made-for-television movies in prime-time program slots. The Fox Broadcasting Company launched what its management claimed was the beginning of a fourth television network, delivering original program series by satellite to independent television stations not affiliated with ABC, CBS, or NBC. Fox management expressed the determination to compete on an equal basis with the three older networks, which had not had to confront an additional network rival since the DuMont Network collapsed thirty years earlier. NBC President Robert C. Wright ("New Universe," 1988, p. 181) observed that "for the first time since DuMont in the '50s, there was an established fourth network, yet the economy seemed barely able to sustain the three it had."

In 1986 the three networks agreed to begin accepting stand alone (not piggy-backed) fifteen-second commercials, exacerbating the clutter problem and adding to the concern of advertisers and their advertising agencies (BBDO, 1986).

The penetration level of videocassette recorders in U.S. television households passed 48.7 percent in 1987, moving in one year from nine percentage points to one percentage point ahead of cable television penetration (Television Bureau of Advertising, 1987b). By January 1988, 48 million households or 53.3 percent of the total owned videocassette recorders (D. Lachenbruch, personal communication, March 23, 1988). By the end of 1987, there were 971 U.S. commercial broadcast television stations in operation, almost 38 percent more than there had been in 1975. The number of stations affiliated with the three major television networks remained about the same (Television Bureau of Advertising, 1987b). Prime-time television viewing dropped an average of four minutes in 1987 from the previous year, a decline that was largely attributed by David Poltrack to the increased use of videocassette recorders to play prerecorded tapes. "The growth of VCRs just about explains the whole decline," he said ("VCRs, People-Meter," 1988). (See Table 3.4 for time spent viewing per TV home—per days 1950–1986.) Poltrack (personal communication, February 4, 1988) said that this pattern was particularly significant on Saturday night (when network viewing is off by 17 percent)

Table 3.4
Time Spent Viewing per TV Home per Day, 1950–1986

	<u>Average Hours per Day</u>
1950	4 hours 35 minutes
1951	4 hours 43 minutes
1952	4 hours 49 minutes
1953	4 hours 40 minutes
1954	4 hours 46 minutes
1955	4 hours 51 minutes
1956	5 hours 1 minute
1957	5 hours 9 minutes
1958	5 hours 5 minutes
1959	5 hours 2 minutes
1960	5 hours 6 minutes
1961	5 hours 7 minutes
1962	5 hours 6 minutes
1963	5 hours 11 minutes
1964	5 hours 25 minutes
1965	5 hours 29 minutes
1966	5 hours 32 minutes
1967	5 hours 42 minutes
1968	5 hours 46 minutes
1969	5 hours 50 minutes
1970	5 hours 56 minutes
1971	6 hours 2 minutes
1972	6 hours 12 minutes
1973	6 hours 15 minutes

1974	6 hours 14 minutes
1975	6 hours 7 minutes
1976	6 hours 18 minutes
1977	6 hours 10 minutes
1978	6 hours 17 minutes
1979	6 hours 28 minutes
1980	6 hours 36 minutes
1981	6 hours 45 minutes
1982	6 hours 48 minutes
1983	7 hours 2 minutes
1984	7 hours 8 minutes
1985	7 hours 10 minutes
1986	7 hours 8 minutes

Source: *Trends in Television*, Television Bureau of Advertising (TvB), (June 1987), p. 7. Reprinted with permission of Television Bureau of Advertising.

and to a lesser extent on Friday nights. He noted that the nights experiencing the least loss of viewers were those on which various studies have indicated the lowest usage of videocassette recorders. Poltrack also observed that since older viewers are the least likely to buy videocassette recorders, NBC's program strategy—positioning *Golden Girls* in the Saturday night prime-time schedule—seems to be well suited to attracting older female audiences, who are less likely to be watching videotaped programing. The vulnerability of the networks was increased after A. C. Nielsen's newly augmented "people meter" technology revealed that prime-time network households ratings were about 10 percent lower than the previous year's, measured by the older passive method ("New TV Ratings Device," 1987).

By May 1989, the three networks' prime-time share of the television audience was 65 percent ("TV, Hollywood Square Off on Fin-Syn," 1989), and plummeted to sixty percent during the summer rerun season as viewers tuned in to cable TV, nonaffiliated independent and public television stations ("TV Network Ratings Fall," 1989). Nielsen research reported that the number of television homes in the United States had grown to more than 90 million in 1988, but the average daily household viewing in that year had dropped to six hours and fifty-five minutes, from seven hours and five minutes the year before ("Daily Viewing Drops," 1989). The research company noted that this was the second consecutive year of decline, but did not offer to explain this trend. In October 1989, it was reported that two major entertainment production companies, MCA and Paramount Communications, were planning to launch a fifth television network which would compete with ABC, CBS, NBC and the Fox Broadcasting Company ("Plan Seen," 1989).

These evolving patterns of television viewing were noted by advertising agency media executives whose judgments can possibly influence its future direction. "The networks are changing the way they do business," said Allen Banks (personal communication, January 20, 1988), executive vice president and director of media at Saatchi & Saatchi USA/DFS Compton. "But even if the networks got down to a 50 percent share of audience, it would still be looked at as the most important way to reach mass audience. The networks will never not exist."

David Bender (personal communication, February 1, 1988), vice president, research, for the advertiser-supported cable television USA Network, observed that the major broadcast networks were being adversely affected by these changes in two ways.

> First, the networks are losing share of audience to the independents [television stations], advertiser-supported cable and pay cable. They're [the major networks] the ones who have the most audience to lose and that's who gets hurt the hardest. Second, they're losing homes using television (HUT) because people are watching their VCRs. I don't think there's anybody who doesn't know that the VCR has made a significant difference.

Larry Cole (personal communication, January 29, 1988), senior vice president and director of media at Ogilvy & Mather, said that the trend of audiences using technological devices to alter their television viewing patterns was of great concern to his industry. "The number of television homes with remote control switchers has risen from almost nothing to a very high percentage." He noted that even if the ratings that measure audience level appear unchanged, "what you're seeing are compensatory audience shifts, where one is shifting in and one is shifting out."

The swift adoption of the videocassette recorder in U.S. television homes has transformed the programing patterns of such pay television networks as Home Box Office (HBO) and Showtime and indirectly contributed to the major broadcast networks' problems of audience erosion, according to Barry Kaplan, vice president of sales and marketing of AGB, a television audience research firm. As owners of videocassette recorders began to rent or buy prerecorded videotapes of movies from retail stores in their neighborhoods, "it caused the pay cable services to change from being completely movie services to much more than that" (B. Kaplan, personal communication, January 18, 1988). The cable services reduced the number of movies they were offering, he said, and began to program live sports and their own originally produced specials. This had the effect of providing another attractive programing alternative to viewers, he concluded, which ultimately caused further erosion of the network audiences.

Network counter-programing practices have played an important role in increasing the use of videocassette recorders in U.S. television homes, and disrupting the traditional network practice of controlling audience flow from one show to the next, said Leo Scullin, senior vice president, director of print and new electronic media at Young & Rubicam. "When two very high quality programs were up against each other, the incidence of taping would go up" (L. Scullin, personal communication, January 26, 1988). "What this was doing was contributing to the use of the VCR. So the VCR phenomenon was kind of aided and abetted by network programing . . . viewers don't have to sit in front of a program that they don't like and wait until another program comes on . . . they've got this control now." Robert C. Wright, president of NBC Television, described the current situation as comparable to being "in the eye of a hurricane" (Sellers, 1988, pp. 115, 122). He forecast "that things are going to get rough," anticipating the inroads of videocassette recorders, cable services, and independent stations would cause network audiences to continue shrinking, "perhaps to as little as 60 percent" (Sellers, 1988, p. 115).

Network television viewing patterns have been increasingly disrupted and modified since the 1970s. The erosion of the network television audience and the disruption of the viewing patterns that were established in the early 1950s were caused by the introduction of a number of new electronic methods of delivering entertainment into American households. These include advertiser-supported cable television, pay television networks, and the home videocassette recorder. These new trends were also precipitated by the expansion and increase in programing power of nonaffiliated independent television stations. The situation has also been exacerbated by the programing practices of the major television networks themselves as they have

Table 3.5
Cable and Pay Cable Households and Penetration 1965–1988

	Cable Households (000)	% of TV Households	Per Cable Households (000)	% of TV Households
1965	1,300	2.3	--	--
1966	1,900	3.3	--	--
1967	2,300	3.9	--	--
1968	2,800	4.7	--	--
1969	3,500	5.7	--	--
1970	3,900	6.7	--	--
1971	4,600	7.7	--	--
1972	5,700	9.2	--	--
1973	6,600	10.2	--	--
1974	7,700	11.6	--	--
1975	8,600	12.6	140	0.2
1976	10,100	14.5	470	0.7
1977	11,200	15.9	980	1.4
1978	12,500	17.1	1,600	2.2
1979	13,600	18.3	3,100	4.2
1980	15,200	19.9	5,200	6.8
1981	17,830	22.3	8,100	10.1
1982	24,290	29.8	12,600	15.5
1983	28,320	34.0	16,160	19.4
1984	32,930	39.3	19,820	23.7
1985	36,340	42.8	21,840	25.7
1986	39,160	45.6	22,840	26.6
1987	41,690	47.7	22,850	26.1
1988	43,790	49.4	24,290	27.4

Source: *Trends in cable TV*, Television Bureau of Advertising (TvB), (1987), p. 3. Reprinted with permission of Television Bureau of Advertising.

increased the fragmentation of their shows with frequent commercial interruptions. And finally, as suggested by Blumler (1986), the concept of a mass audience for general interest programing may be losing its viability.

(See Table 3.5 for cable and pay cable penetration from 1965 to 1988. See Table 3.6 for annual total network TV audience share 1975 to 1989.)

Table 3.6
Annual Total Network Television Share of Audience 1975–1989

Year	Daypart	
	Daytime	Primetime
1975–76	81%	89%
1976–77	81	91
1977–78	78	91
1978–79	77	90
1979–80	75	87
1980–81	73	84
1981–82	69	80
1982–83	67	77
1983–84	65	76
1984–85	62	73
1985–86	61	73
1986–87	60	71
1987–88	60	71
1988–89	57	63

Source: *A. C. Neilsen media research television audience report, 1975–1989.* A. C. Neilsen, (1975–1989).
Note: Figures are for October-August of each year.

4

The National Television
Advertiser

The three major U.S. broadcast television networks (ABC, CBS, and NBC Television Networks) were nurtured and shaped by national advertisers who were seeking new and more potent methods to engage the loyalties and pocketbooks of the American public. These networks are still engaged in the fundamental business of "the selling of eyeballs to advertisers domestically" ("NBC's Aggressive Foreign Agenda," 1989).

The videocassette recorder was introduced to America in the 1970s primarily as a time-shift mechanism which would allow television enthusiasts to either videotape network TV programs while they were away from home, or to tape one network show while watching another being telecast at the same time.

Without advertisers, the VCR would never have been successfully adopted as a consumer technology in the United States. For this reason, an analysis of the influence and continuing impact of national advertisers is incorporated in this text.

ORIGINS

In 1964 network television advertising patterns were still growing from roots established by radio networks in the late 1920s. Starting in 1927 with NBC's two networks, broadcasting companies initiated the tradition of selling sponsorships of network programs to advertisers. This began even though the Radio Act of 1927 (established by the U.S. government to control the behavior of the commercial radio networks) did not specifically allow for a commercial broadcasting system.

Earlier attempts to commercialize the new medium had been condemned by many public figures, including Herbert Hoover and H.G. Wells. To nullify such criticism, AT&T, which had originated the concept of network broadcasting (and which was subsequently forced by the federal government to withdraw from the broadcasting business), agreed that "it was against the public interest to broadcast pure advertising matter" (Barnouw, 1978, p. 15). This policy position was modified by AT&T's successors and ultimately forgotten as the fledgling radio networks experienced economic difficulties when Wall Street collapsed in 1929.

Although NBC had initially banned advertising of specific brand name products and refused advertisers access to its airwaves between 7 P.M. and 11 P.M., both NBC and newcomer CBS were soon accepting advertising that incorporated blatant promotional material. Broadcast advertising of a product's price was allowed first on the CBS radio network. An American Tobacco commercial proclaimed, "Cremo Cigars only cost 5 cents." This same radio spot promoted some questionable product attributes ("There is no spit in Cremo"). Radio eventually became the preferred advertising medium for dozens of drug companies, offering patent medicine potions and cures of debatable value (Barnouw, 1978, pp. 13, 22, 25–26).

While the overall U.S. economy suffered in the years following the stock market crash in 1929, network radio was built into a profitable business in the early 1930s by revenues derived from a growing number of national advertisers. The benefits of this remarkable new medium as an innovative and potent selling vehicle had quickly become apparent: Radio could reach large groups of people at the same time. Until the advent of radio, advertisers had to rely largely on newspapers and magazines (which were experienced individually rather than en masse) to communicate their persuasive messages. When radio speakers replaced headsets in the 1920s, entire families could collectively share a media experience which previously had been an individual one (Fox, 1984, pp. 150–52).

From the broadcasters' point of view, radio listening had only one purpose: the delivery of audiences to advertisers willing to pay them for the privilege of pitching their products. William S. Paley, the first president of CBS, characterized his network as "the largest advertising medium in the world." Such broadcasters as Paley concurred that their networks' programing was merely a means to a highly profitable end. CBS set the pace in the early 1930s, as radio networks changed their role from electronic purveyors of culture to sellers of audiences to advertisers (Bergreen, 1980, p. 8).

As their radio audiences swelled across the United States, network managements were forced to confront the increasingly difficult task of producing large amounts of quality programing on a daily basis. Confounded by the enormous amount of air time they were required to fill, they turned to their large advertisers for help. The advertisers in turn submitted this challenge to their advertising agencies. These major New York agencies soon became the primary suppliers of programing for the radio networks, a process that eventually saw the advertisers, through their agencies, taking nearly complete control of most network radio shows. Agencies created shows for a single advertiser to sponsor. That advertiser then controlled most aspects of its show's presentation. The networks increasingly behaved as common carriers, providing national advertisers with broadcast conduits through which they could fulfill their marketing needs (Heighton and Cunningham, 1976, pp. 11–12).

National advertisers dominated the network radio broadcasting industry for the next three decades, maintaining their power and influence through the combined use of financial muscle and their advertising agencies' creative talents. With the collaboration of the networks' managements, they skillfully linked the names of their companies and their products with the names and identities of popular stars and shows. For example, Wheaties, "the Breakfast of Champions," was closely associated with *Jack Armstrong, the All-American Boy*. This highly rated adventure series, sponsored by General Mills, premiered on network radio in 1933 and continued for the next eighteen years (p. 17).

Through the 1930s until the beginning of World War II, a tone of aggressive salesmanship permeated network radio advertising. For the duration of the war, however, that hard-selling tone was softened. National advertisers, primarily involved in producing goods for the government, used network radio as a way to maintain and improve their corporate images. At the cessation of hostilities in 1945, major advertisers refocused their attention on the consumer market and resumed the use of network radio to stimulate demand for their products and services (Barnouw, 1978, pp. 37–41). (See Table 4.1 for comparison of network radio and television advertising expenditures 1935–1982.)

THE BEGINNING OF NATIONAL TELEVISION ADVERTISING

The commercial possibilities of television were being explored at the same time commercial radio was launched in the United States. RCA's

Table 4.1
Advertiser Expenditures in Broadcasting: Network Radio and Television, 1935–1982 (all dollar figures in millions)

Year	Network Radio Advertising	Network Television Advertising
1935	$ 63	N/A
1936	75	
1937	89	
1938	89	
1939	99	
1940	113	
1941	125	
1942	129	
1943	157	
1944	192	
1945	198	
1946	200	
1947	201	
1948	211	
1949	203	$ 30
1950	196	85
1951	180	181
1952	162	256
1953	141	320
1954	114	422
1955	84	550
1956	60	643
1957	63	690
1958	58	742
1959	44	776
1960	43	820
1961	43	887
1962	46	976
1963	56	1,025
1964	59	1,132
1965	60	1,237
1966	63	1,393
1967	64	1,455
1968	63	1,523
1969	59	1,678
1970	56	1,658
1971	63	1,593
1972	74	1,804
1973	68	1,968
1974	69	2,145
1975	83	2,306
1976	105	2,857
1977	137	3,460
1978	147	3,975
1979	161	4,599
1980	183	5,130
1981	230	5,575
1982	255	6,210

Source: C.H. Sterling, *Electronic media: A guide to trends in broadcasting and media technologies 1920–1983*. New York: Praeger (1984), pp. 83, 84, 85. Reprinted with permission of Praeger.

David Sarnoff was proposing the development of television as an advertising medium as early as 1923. In 1927 Sarnoff predicted "the imminence of television's arrival" (Bergreen, 1980, p. 7). In 1931, advertising executive Edgar Felix wrote:

> The cigar manufacturer who appeals to young men can actually demonstrate [on television] that cigar smoking will make any young man look like a major executive.... [A] reproduction of a luscious strawberry shortcake [will be] much more effective in creating an appetite than any word-of-mouth description. Television, because of its ability to illustrate and dramatize an advertiser's message, is destined to become the most powerful medium for sales stimulation. (Adler, 1981, p. 267)

Agnew and O'Brien (1958, p. 2) stated that television advertising in the United States actually began at 8 A.M. on July 1, 1941, with a live Bulova (watch) time signal over NBC's New York television station WNBT. The first network television commercial, sponsored by Gillette (shaving products), was broadcast by WNBT on June 19, 1946, during the telecast of the Louis-Conn heavyweight championship boxing match from Yankee Stadium in the Bronx: It was carried by four stations. RCA and other companies that were broadcasters as well as manufacturers of television receivers moved quickly on both fronts to take maximum advantage of the anticipated consumer demand. Television sets with small screens (eight to ten inches), costing between $300 and $500, sold briskly in every market where television signals were received. This tremendous demand, exploding after years of material deprivation during the war, was reflected in virtually every other aspect of the consumer market. Major national advertisers and their advertising agencies began preparing to make the transition to this new medium, with the complete support of the networks' managements (Heighton and Cunningham, 1976, p. 25).

Both Reel (1979, p. 5) and Sterling and Kittross (1978, p. 271) observed that the transition happened faster and with greater ease than many in the radio network business had expected because most of the economic and operating patterns of television were anticipated and pioneered by radio. Advertisers, either directly or through their advertising agencies, began to produce most of the programs, as well as all of the commercials. This method of working had been well established in radio since the 1930s; it was comfortable and profitable for both the sponsors and the networks. Advertisers would take their programs to one of the networks and pay for the time charges involved in putting their shows, along with their commercials, on the air. In the early years of television, network managements were happy to retain this arrangement.

Some cautious network executives initially believed that the significantly higher cost of producing shows and commercials for television would act as a brake on advertisers, causing them to make a more gradual transition from radio to television during the 1950s. In 1949 one industry study expressed "serious doubt that television will ever become a truly nationwide medium (as compared with present radio patterns and service) if it has to depend on the economics of advertising alone" (Sterling and Kittross, 1978, p. 271). While the majority of the large national advertisers plunged enthusiastically into the new medium, some advertisers and advertising agencies initially shied away from television because of its high cost or, at least, approached it with caution. But by the 1951–1952 television season, the majority of the nation's large national advertisers had started to abandon network radio as a primary mass-medium vehicle; radio was becoming a dying operation. The stampede from radio to television was abetted by hundreds of ambitious and talented radio executives who rapidly decided to further their careers by switching their allegiances from radio to television.

Sterling (1984, p. 272) noted that in 1949, the first year that network television made enough money to be measured, the medium earned a total of only $30 million in advertising revenues; network radio earned $203 million. A year later, network television earned $85 million and network radio earned $196 million. In 1951, network television earned $181 million, passing network radio's earnings of $180 million. A year later, network television earned $256 million and network radio's earnings had been reduced further to $162 million. Through the remainder of the 1950s, network television's earnings from advertising revenues continued to climb, reaching $776 million in 1959, while network radio's income from advertising continued to plummet to $44 million in the same year. Many national advertisers who embraced television in its early stages of development benefited spectacularly. For example, Heighton and Cunningham (1976, p. 26) stated that Hazel Bishop, a small cosmetics company producing only $50,000 a year in sales, invested its entire advertising budget in television in 1950. By 1952, the company's sales had reached $4.5 million.

Advertising agencies that anticipated the explosive growth potential of the new medium and positioned themselves to exploit its benefits grew just as quickly. According to Fox (1984, p. 210), BBDO was one such agency. By 1950, the BBDO television department had grown from 12 employees to 150 and it was placing $4 million in television for its clients. In three years during the early 1950s, the

Chicago-based Leo Burnett agency saw its clients' billings in television grow from 18 percent to more than 50 percent. By 1959, Benton & Bowles, a New York advertising agency that initially had been somewhat skeptical about television's prospects for rapid growth, was earning 60 percent of its revenues from the placement of clients' commercials on television. During this period, "The Golden Age of Television," the advertising agencies and their sponsor-clients totally dominated network television's creative and programing arena. Such dramatic shows as *Kraft Television Theater, Goodyear TV Playhouse* and *Texaco Star Theatre*, which enjoyed long runs on the air and won many awards, were delivered to the networks complete. Networks had only to provide facilities, air time, and occasionally exercise the right of censorship.

A fundamental marketing discovery fueled the enthusiasm of national advertisers to "own" their clearly identifiable programs. Reel (1979, p. 6) related that Peter Levathes, a broadcast industry executive, testified at an FCC committee hearing in 1959 that advertisers were beginning to consider factors other than high audience ratings in selecting shows with which they would be identified. "Even though an advertiser is up against a "strong" program on another network, he may well be satisfied with a smaller audience if he is reaching the type of audience to whom his product is salable," Levathes said. His testimony pointed to a new awareness by television advertisers of demographic information which was beginning to influence them and their advertising agencies. This awareness caused both groups to question whether having access to large numbers of people should be the sole criterion for investing in programing, and in the use of the television medium itself. Nobody could deny that network television was the most powerful tool ever devised for the purpose of delivering massive groups of Americans to advertisers for exposure to their sales messages. But advertisers and their agencies began to wonder if all of these viewers were actually prospective customers for their particular products or services. This question was raised with growing intensity for the next twenty years until it surfaced as the cause of a major economic crisis for the networks in the late 1970s, possibly leading to their gradual loss of power, and eventual decline.

When advertisers and agency influence over network television's programing content and practices became most powerful in the late 1950s, the U.S. attorney general and the FCC began to express concern about the television industry's possible abrogation of responsibility. In a report to the president in 1959 (Barnouw, 1978, p. 53), the attorney general explained that affiliated television stations were "legally responsible" for what they broadcast. The networks, however, were responsible for most of the programing that was broadcast by the local stations, and the networks had sold this control of programing to national advertisers and their advertising agencies. According to Barnouw (p. 58), the concern reached crisis proportions late in 1959 when Charles Van Doren, a contestant on a highly rated network television quiz show called *The $64,000 Question*, acknowledged that he had been given answers in advance. Subsequent investigation revealed that the show's sponsor, Revlon Cosmetics, had influenced a large number of additional contestants and others associated with the production of the popular show to lie to a grand jury about their involvement in this matter. The angry reaction of Congress and the FCC to these revelations forced the three networks to begin a massive reorganization of their program development procedures. Consequently, similar quiz shows were taken off the air, and the network managements began taking steps to demonstrate to the public that television was an industry with integrity, capable of controlling its own programing schedules. The stage was set for a dramatic shift in the balance of power from the advertising community to the networks and this shift has kept primary programing power in the networks' hands until the present.

For the first time in their history, the ABC, CBS, and NBC television networks took control over their program development and scheduling operations, almost completely removing the advertisers and their agencies from the process. This represented an abrupt transition from the networks' long-held position of reliance on advertisers to provide them with most of the programing they fed to their affiliated stations. Further, the networks drastically reduced the opportunities for advertisers to be the single sponsor of continuing dramatic or comedy series, initiating instead the concept of buying participations in many different shows. As described by DeLuca (1980, pp. 130–31), this change was caused by economic pressures as much as by the desire of network management to regain control of programing. Beginning in the late 1950s, the costs of producing shows for network television had become increasingly expensive, making programing progressively more difficult for advertisers to underwrite by themselves. Large agencies, such as J. Walter Thompson Company, frequently acted as brokers, arranging cosponsorships among their clients so that these costs and the commercial time could be more easily divided.

Many of the concepts affecting fragmented network television sponsorships were pioneered by NBC president Sylvester L. "Pat" Weaver (Heighton and Cunningham, 1976, p. 29). Among other innovative ideas, he introduced the magazine format on which the *Today* and *Tonight* shows were based. This format allowed advertisers with limited budgets to air single commercials, without investing the large sums that had previously been necessary to sponsor traditionally produced shows. The obvious advantage of providing more cost efficiency and greater reach (exposure to different households) by delivering an advertiser's commercial messages over a wider variety of shows and dayparts (times of the programing day) was a compelling argument to many advertisers who had previously been wedded to the idea of single-show sponsorship. This was particularly true of such large packaged goods companies as Procter & Gamble, which were more interested in assuring television exposure for their hundreds of different branded products than for their corporate identities.

Following the quiz show scandals of 1959–1960, the trend toward buying participations, rather than single sponsorships, on network television became inexorable as advertisers responded to a combination of network pressure and a desire to get more diverse exposure for their advertising dollars. According to Barnouw (1978, p. 151), this dramatic shift from national advertisers' involvement in single-sponsored shows to multiple participations produced significant changes both in the way the networks sold commercial time and in the structure of the programing itself. To allow for greater flexibility in scheduling advertisers' television spots, the networks began selling six one-minute insertions in each hour of prime-time programing. Subsequently they allowed these gaps in their programs to be divided still further into twelve thirty-second commercials.

Of economic necessity, the form of network dramatic and comedy shows began to be characterized as highly episodic, with new openings and climaxes every seven or eight minutes. As this new program formula evolved into a formal network mode, it exacerbated the already growing problem of clutter. It also established a precedent which, many years later, encouraged the networks to provide themselves with even greater commercial scheduling flexibility by allowing fifteen-second commercials, thereby compounding the problems of commercial saturation and viewer annoyance.

Some national advertisers pursued their corporate visions of program quality and diversity into the early 1960s, according to Fox (1984, p. 213). But the shows they supported, such as the *Voice of Firestone*, *Armstrong Circle Theater*, and the *Alcoa-Goodyear Playhouse*, were eventually canceled by the networks even though their sponsors were satisfied and wanted to continue paying the costs of having them on the air. The network managements, supported by ratings data supplied by A. C. Nielsen, were now pursuing mass audiences and were determined to maintain total control of the medium. The new network philosophy also put them in conflict with sophisticated national advertisers who were becoming more focused on their prime customer prospects and were unwilling to pay to have their commercials exposed to viewers whom they considered less desirable. Sterling and Kittross (1978, p. 354) report that these advertisers demanded even more specific demographic data from the networks about the age, sex, income, and other factors concerning the viewers of each network television show.

Advertiser determination to spend only in pursuit of their most desirable target audiences (typically women, ages eighteen to forty-nine) eventually influenced the networks to begin canceling some of their highest rated shows because their audiences were either too young, too old, or were living in rural areas. Shows with large audiences such as *The Beverly Hillbillies* and *Bonanza*, were replaced by others specifically designed to attract younger, more urban viewers who could be more easily sold to advertisers.

NETWORK TELEVISION ADVERTISING FROM 1964 TO 1975

U.S. advertisers spent more than $14 billion in 1964 in all media. Total television advertising volume was $2.9 billion. Of that amount, $1.1 billion went to the three broadcast television networks. The remaining broadcast dollars that year were spent in spot and local television markets. More than three-quarters of the commercials on network television were sixty-second spots; the remaining availabilities were filled with "piggy-backs" which are two different, consecutive thirty-second commercials purchased by the same company, sometimes advertising the same brand and sometimes a different brand (Television Bureau of Advertising, 1987b, pp. 10, 11, 14). The 125 leading national advertisers surveyed by *Advertising Age* (the foremost advertising trade magazine) reported that they had spent a total of almost $979 million in network television advertising in 1964, or more than 85 percent of the total amount spent in the medium. P & G was the number one national advertiser that year, posting total billings of $225 million. This company also ranked first in network television spending in 1964, allocating more than $78 million (almost twice as much as second-ranked American Home Products Corp.) ("Top 125 National Advertisers Spent $3.8 billion" 1965).

In 1968, U.S. advertisers spent a total of $18.1 billion, an increase of 28 percent over 1964. National advertisers spent $3.6 billion in all forms of commercial television, 57 percent more than was spent five years previously. Network television advertising revenues for 1968 amounted to $1.5 billion, an increase of $391 million over 1964. All other television dollars were spent in spot and local categories. By 1968, only 40 percent of the commercials on network television were sixty seconds, cutting by almost half the number of that length aired in 1964. More than 50 percent of all commercials on network television were piggy-backed, with free-standing thirty-second spots accounting for the remainder (Television Bureau of Advertising, 1987b, pp. 10–11, 14). *Advertising Age* reported that the top 125 national advertisers had increased their spending in network television to $1.3 billion in 1968, an increase over the previous five-year period of $332 million, or 34 percent. This group of advertisers accounted for 84.7 percent of all money spent on network television, approximately the same as in 1964. With a network appropriation of $100.8 million in 1968, P & G continued to be the biggest advertiser on the medium (although it reduced its investment by $12 million from the previous year). In 1968 the second largest network television advertiser was Bristol-Myers, with $49.7 million spent in network television ("Top 125 National Advertisers Put Record $4.83 Billion," 1969).

In 1973, total advertising volume in the United States was almost $25 billion, an increase of 29 percent over 1968. Total television advertising during that year was $4.5 billion, an increase of 24 percent over 1968. Network television advertising volume in 1973 was almost $2 billion, an increase of only 17 percent. All other money spent on television advertising went into spot and local areas. Only 8.5 percent of all commercials on network television were sixty-second spots; 72 percent were stand-alone thirty-second spots; and the remainder were piggy-back (Television Bureau of Advertising, 1987b). The impact of the Arab oil embargo in the fall of 1973 forced substantial advertising budget cutbacks by the largest U.S. oil companies. Nevertheless, the top 100 advertisers (Advertising Age had reduced the number of companies in its annual study from 125 to 100 in 1970) still accounted for $1.6 billion, or 76 percent of all dollars spent on network television. In 1973, P & G continued to lead all other advertisers in network television expenditures, increasing its investment in the medium by 29 percent from $100.8 million in 1969 to $129.3 million. American Home Products and Bristol-Myers were virtually tied for second position, each spending about $70.5 million in network television that year ("Top 100 National Advertisers Hike Ad Total to $5.68 Billion," 1974).

NETWORK ADVERTISING FROM 1975 TO THE PRESENT

In 1975, the year in which Sony introduced the Betamax videocassette recorder to the United States, advertisers spent $5.3 billion in all forms of television, up 18 percent in the two-year period. Advertisers were now investing 18.9 percent of all advertising dollars in television, an increase of 2.7 percent since 1964. By 1975, there were 513 advertisers using network television to promote 2,132 different branded products. In 1970 (the first year for which these data were presented by the Television Bureau of Advertising), 427 advertisers had used network television to promote 2,348 brands. Advertisers spent $2.3 billion on network television in 1975, increasing their 1973 investment by more than 17 percent. By this time, only 5.6 percent of all network television commercials were sixty-second spots; 79 percent were thirty seconds and the remainder were piggy-backs (Television Bureau of Advertising, 1987b). The 100 leading national advertisers spent $1.9 billion on network television in 1975, an investment increase of more than $300 million since 1973. Their network television spending still accounted for slightly more than 76 percent of network advertising expenditures. P & G had increased its lead as the number one network television advertiser, committing $32 million over its 1973 allocation; this represented an increase of almost 25 percent over 1973 spending levels. Bristol-Myers was second, having spent $89.7 million during that year ("Top 100 Advertisers Hike Total to $6.3 Billion," 1976).

Advertising spending in the United States accelerated dramatically during the five-year period between 1975 and 1980 (increasing 92 percent to $53.6 billion). Television advertising investments more than doubled during this interval, jumping to $11.4 billion. The amount devoted to network advertising grew even faster, increasing more than 200 percent to $5.1 billion in 1980.

It was the first year that advertisers invested enough in national syndication (programs distributed on a station-by-station basis, as opposed to simultaneous, electronic distribution to a large group of affiliated stations, as is done by the networks) to justify the Television Bureau of Advertising's reporting on this revenue. It was also the first year that advertising revenues generated by cable television were sizable enough to be noted. While the actual dollar amounts involved were relatively small (in 1980, $50 million was earned in national syndication and $58 million in cable television), they were an indication that the commercial broadcast television networks were being confronted by increasing competition for national advertiser dollars.

The thirty-second format was being used by 94.6 percent of all network television advertisers by 1980. Only 1.9 percent of network television spots that year were sixty seconds. In addition, other commercial lengths, such as ten-second, forty-five-second, and ninety-second spots were emerging, although not to any significant degree (Television Bureau of Advertising, 1987b, pp. 10–11, 14).

The 100 leading U.S. advertisers invested $3.9 billion in network television in 1980, representing 75.7 percent of the total in all advertising. This was an increase of almost 91 percent from the amount invested in the medium in 1975. Leading advertiser P & G bought $361.1 million worth of commercial time on the three television networks during that year, more than doubling what it spent in 1975. The next largest network television spender was General Foods, investing $201.5 million in 1980 ("100 Leaders," 1981).

Total U.S. advertising volume in 1985 was $94.8 billion, an increase of 77 percent over the previous five-year period. The rate of television advertising volume grew even more for the five-year period, rising 80 percent to $20.5 billion.

Advertisers spent $8.3 billion on network television in 1985, increasing the rate of their investment by 62 percent compared to 1980. Other television advertising categories gained even more during this five-year time frame. National spot television advertising (sold by the national sales representatives of individual television stations as ad hoc networks) increased 84 percent to $6 billion; local television advertising (sold locally by individual television stations) went up 93 percent to $5.7 billion; and national syndication advertising grew more than 500 percent to an estimated $540 million.

Cable television advertising revenues had increased dramatically during the five-year period, from $58 million to $751 million. These figures offered indisputable evidence that national advertisers were pursuing the multiple viewing options available to American television watchers. The variety of television commercial formats had broadened between 1980 and 1985. A little more than 2 percent of all commercials were sixty seconds long, 1.3 percent were ten seconds, 10.1 percent were fifteen seconds, 83.5 percent were thirty seconds, 1.4 percent were forty-five seconds, and fewer than .5 percent were ninety seconds or longer (Television Bureau of Advertising, 1987a, p. 7; 1987b, pp. 10–11, 14).

The 100 leading national advertisers spent $6.3 billion in network television in 1985, an increase of 63 percent from the 1980 figure. The 1985 investment represented a reduction of 2.6 percent from the previous year's commitment. These top advertisers continued to control more than three-quarters of all commercial spending on network television. P & G retained its primary position, dispersing $488.8 million (an increase of 35 percent over the sum invested in 1980). The second largest advertiser in network television was Philip Morris Companies, which spent $348.3 million in 1985 ("Advertisers Cut," 1986).

National advertisers passed the $100 billion mark in 1986, spending almost four times more than they had in 1975. A total of $22 billion in advertising was invested in television in 1986, a sum almost three and one-half times greater than that spent in 1975. Television advertising was now accounting for 21.8 percent of all U.S. advertising dollars. It accounted for 18.9 percent in 1975 and 16.2 percent in 1964.

Network television advertising totalled $8.6 billion in 1986. This amount was almost four times more than that spent in 1975 and more than seven times larger than expenditures in 1964. While these figures appeared to represent substantial growth, they were shadowed by alternative forms of television competing for a part of the advertising pie. National spot television advertising was $6.6 billion, more than four times larger than in 1975, and more than eight times greater than in 1964. Local television advertising was also about $6.6 billion, having increased nearly five times since 1975, and almost nineteen times since 1964. National syndication advertising was estimated to have totalled $610 million in 1986, more than twelve times as much as when it was first reported by the Television Bureau of Advertising in 1980. Cable television earned $930 million in 1986, sixteen times more than was reported in 1980, the first year it accrued sufficient revenues to be measured. By 1986, 20.9 percent of all commercials aired on the networks were fifteen-second spots and 73.6 percent were of thirty-second duration; all other formats were less than 2 percent.

There were 638 advertisers utilizing network television in 1986, 24 percent more than used the medium in 1975 (Television Bureau of Advertising, 1987a, p. 7; 1987b, pp. 10–11, 14–15). The 100 leading national advertisers spent $6.4 billion in network television in 1986, accounting for 74 percent of all advertising dollars invested in the medium. While these advertisers committed only a little more money to network television in 1986 than in the previous year, the sum represented a slightly smaller share of the total advertising dollars spent by the group. Spot television increased its share of the total in 1986. P & G remained the leading advertiser on network television, investing $456.3 million that year, but it reduced its commitment from the previous year by 7 percent as it reallocated its total budget into other promotional areas (e.g., direct marketing and couponing). In 1987 the Cincinnati-based company further reduced its network television spending by $75 million, or 16.4 percent, the greatest annual cut in network television advertising in the company's history. Industry analysts suggested that the reason for the company's decision to slash its network spending was largely based on declining efficiencies in network television advertising caused by excessive pricing. Cable television, national syndication, and such sales promotion areas as couponing were believed to be the main beneficiaries of this budget diversion ("P & G Cut $75 million," 1988, pp. 1, 73). This pattern was beginning to be emulated by other leading advertisers acting on their growing concern about such issues as the rising cost of advertising on network television, the impact of clutter on viewers' attentiveness, and the continuing problem of network audience erosion, as well as a desire to achieve greater measurability of the results of advertising spending ("Ad Growth," 1987). (Table 4.2 shows network and cable television advertising volume from their earliest years of measurement.)

Cable television appeared to be the medium benefiting most directly from network television's troubles. As cable penetration reached 50 percent of all U.S. television households, national advertisers began reallocating dollars, previously committed to network television, into such advertiser-supported cable television networks as ESPN, MTV, WTBS, and USA Network. As network television's advertising costs rose and its audience shrank, some advertisers sought cable television as a more cost-efficient way to promote their products and services. Cable television advertising revenues grew rapidly in 1987 ("Cable TV Ad Sales," 1987, p. 2). Advertising revenues for all cable networks grew 28 percent to $2.6 billion and the seventeen largest cable networks' revenues increased 60 percent ("Suddenly, Basic Cable," 1988).

Some observers believe that the shifts of advertising money from network television to cable was engineered by U.S. advertising agencies who were determined "to break the hegemony of the broadcast networks." According to Edward Ney, former chairman of the Young & Rubicam agency, frustrated advertisers wanted the same wide selection of promotional alternatives available to them as they had in newspapers, magazines, and radio stations. Resenting the power that the three broadcast television networks had to demand—and get—double-digit price increases each year, the advertisers, through their major agencies, began devoting larger percentages of their television budgets to advertising on cable networks. "Now if advertisers balk at broadcast network [advertising] increases, CNN, ESPN, and other established cable networks are viable, realistically priced alternatives with sufficient viewers for advertiser needs," said Ron Kaatz, former senior vice president and director of media concepts for J. Walter Thompson Company ("Cable: Billion-Dollar Baby," 1987).

Advertisers were also becoming concerned about the proliferation of videocassette recorders in American homes and the new technology's ability to liberate television viewers from scheduling their daily routines around the network time slots assigned to their favorite programs. The acknowledged tendency of VCR viewers to avoid commercials in previously taped popular television shows by "zipping" through them was causing considerable advertiser anxiety. The increased use of remote control channel selectors, with which viewers skipped across the television spectrum while commercials were airing, furthered advertisers' distress with the traditional television medium ("Cable Eroding," 1986). It motivated one of the industry's largest advertising agencies, Ted Bates, to send an itemized bill to each of the three networks for the portion of its clients' buys

Table 4.2
Television Advertising Volume (in millions)

	Network	Cable
1950	$ 85	N/A to 1980
1951	181	
1952	256	
1953	320	
1954	422	
1955	550	
1956	643	
1957	690	
1958	742	
1959	776	
1960	820	
1961	887	
1962	976	
1963	1,025	
1964	1,132	
1965	1,237	
1966	1,393	
1967	1,455	
1968	1,523	
1969	1,678	
1970	1,658	
1971	1,593	
1972	1,804	
1973	1,968	
1974	2,145	
1975	2,306	
1976	2,857	
1977	3,460	
1978	3,975	
1979	4,599	
1980	5,130	$ 85
1981	5,575	122
1982	6,210	227
1983	7,107	353
1984	8,526	572
1985	8,285	751
1986	8,579	930
1987	8,830	1,142
1988	N/A	1,395a

Source: *Trends in television*, Television Bureau of Advertising (TvB), (1987), p. 11. *Trends in cable*, Television Bureau of Advertising (TvB), (1987), p. 7. Reprinted with permission of Television Bureau of Advertising.

(for one quarter in 1985) that the agency estimated was lost to videocassette recording. The networks either ignored this initiative or suggested that the portion of the commercial audience lost due to videocassette recorders was insignificant ("Bates Bullies Nets," 1986). The debate over this issue continues. Advertising agency president Ronald K. Sherman (1987) warned that the American television viewer is taking control of television: "armed with a remote channel switcher and a VCR, he or she represents the single greatest threat the advertising medium has ever known" (p. 30).

In an apparent replay of the 1950s and early 1960s, advertisers and their agencies have begun demonstrating interest in producing programing which would allow them to regain control of the environment in which their commercials are viewed as well as to manage costs more effectively ("Advertisers get into the Act," 1989).

The networks have further exhibited their new willingness to create a friendlier environment for advertisers by offering availabilities for placement of branded products in situation comedies and dramas ("Networks Push," 1988). While the three networks recorded $9.6 billion in sales in 1988, an increase of 8.7 percent over the previous year ("Ad Spending," 1989), many national advertisers expressed increasing concern about the medium's ability to reach their customers on a cost-effective basis. Chrysler Corporation, previously one of the largest national advertisers on network television, announced in October 1989 that it was shifting 70 percent of its media budget into print to support the launch of its 1990 model year. The previous year, the auto maker had committed 60 percent of its budget to television, with only 40 percent dedicated to print media ("Chrysler-Brand Media," 1989).

KEY INFORMANT SURVEY OF TOP 100 NATIONAL ADVERTISERS

To determine the attitudes of leading national advertisers toward the videocassette recorder and its impact on network viewing patterns and network television advertising, a brief questionnaire was mailed to senior marketing or advertising executives in each of the 100 leading network advertising companies (representing more than 75 percent of all U.S. advertising dollars invested in network television). (See Table 4.3 for list of top 100 advertisers sent questionnaire.) The key informant method described by Phillips (1981), a technique of collecting information by interviewing informants who have a particular status or specialized knowledge about a subject, was utilized. Data were collected from executive informants in the 100 American corporations identified in the January-September 1987 Broadcast

Table 4.3
Top 100 National Advertisers Sent Questionnaire

Rank	Company
1	Procter & Gamble Co.
2	Philip Morris Companies Inc.
3	Kellogg Co.
4	Unilever MV
5	General Motors Corp.
6	McDonalds Corp.
7	RJR Nabisco Inc.
8	Johnson & Johnson
9	American Home Products Corp.
10	Annheuser-Busch Cos. Inc.

Top 10 total

Rank	Company
11	Ford Motor Co.
12	Mars Inc.
13	Pepsico Inc.
14	Chrysler Corp.
15	Bristol-Myers Co.
16	American Telephone & Telegraph Co.
17	Coca-Cola Co.
18	General Mills Inc.
19	Sterling Drug Inc.
20	Warner-Lambert Co.
21	Nestle SA
22	Ralston Purina Co.
23	Pillsbury Co.
24	Sears Roebuck & Co.
25	Quaker Oats Co.

Top 25 total

Rank	Company
26	American Dairy Association
27	Honda Motor Co. Ltd.
28	Colgate-Palmolive Co.
29	American Express Co.
30	Kraft Inc.
31	Schering-Plough Corp.
32	Dow Chemical Co.
33	Beecham Group PLC
34	Wrighley Wm Jr. Co.
35	Gallo E & J Winery
36	ITOH C & Co. Ltd.
37	Moxell Corp.
38	Wendy's International Inc.
39	Coors Adolph Co.
40	Eastman Kodak Co.
41	Clorox Co.

42	U.S. Government
43	International Business Machine Corp.
44	BCI Holdings Corp.
45	Mennen Co.
46	Heinz HJ Co.
47	Nissan Motor Co. Ltd.
48	Bayer AG
49	Volkswagenwerk AG
50	General Electric Co.

Top 50 total

51	Sara Lee Corp.
52	Prudential Insurance Co. of America
53	Hicks & Haas
54	Penney JC Co. Inc.
55	Campbell Soup Co.
56	US Sprint Communications Co.
57	Monsanto Co.
58	Stroh Brewery Co.
59	Metropolitan Life Insurance Co.
60	Kimberly-Clark Corp.
61	Pfizer Inc.
62	Toyota Motor Corp.
63	Allegis Corp.
64	Hallmark Cards Inc.
65	Helene Curtis Industries
66	AMR Corp.
67	Cosmair Inc.
68	Dominos Pizza Inc.
69	Bayerische Motoren Werke Aktiengesellsch
70	United Biscuits (Holdings) PLC
71	American Cyanamid Co.
72	Johnson SC & Sons Inc.
73	Fuji Heavy Industries Inc. Ltd.
74	Hershey Foods Corp.
75	Dupont de Nemours EI & Co. Inc.

Top 75 total

76	First Brands Corp.
77	Seagram Co. Ltd.
78	Revlon Group Inc.
79	Playtex Inc.
80	Gillette Co.
81	Reckitt & Colman PLC
82	Welcome Foundation Ltd
83	Carter-Wallace Inc.
84	United Parcel Service of America Inc.

Table 4.3 (continued)

85	North American Philips Corp.
86	Canandaigua Wine Co. Inc.
87	Thompson Medical Co. Inc.
88	Alberto-Culver Co.
89	Tambrands
90	CPC International Inc.
91	Whirlpool Corp.
92	Daimler-Benz AG
93	Block Drug Co. Inc.
94	Tandy Corp.
95	Tri-Star PIctures
96	MCA Inc.
97	Merrill Lynch & Co. Inc.
98	Quaker State Corp.
99	Castle & Cooke Inc.
100	Canon Inc.

Source: *BAR/LNA multi-media service report*, (January-September 1987)

Advertisers Reports, Inc. *(BAR)/Leading National Advertisers (LNA) Service Report* as the 100 leading network television advertisers. This source was cross-referenced against the 1987 edition of *Advertising Age's 100 Leading National Advertisers*. Specific names, corporate titles, and addresses were verified in the October 1987 edition of the *Standard Directory of Advertisers*. In each targeted company, the highest level executive with either an advertising, a marketing, or media title was selected to be the respondent. A self-addressed, stamped envelope was enclosed to maximize the return rate. Fifty-one percent of all those surveyed completed and returned the questionnaire. Sixteen were marketing executives and thirty-five were advertising or media executives.

SUMMARY OF RESPONSES TO QUESTIONNAIRE

1. Did you react in 1987 to the continuing erosion of prime-time network audience share (currently at 72 percent) by reallocating portions of your network television advertising budget to other media?

Seventy-one percent of the national advertisers who responded indicated that they had reacted in 1987 to the continuing erosion of prime-time network television audience share by reallocating (to other media) a portion of the budget they had previously allocated to network television. Of the 71 percent, almost 14 percent volunteered that they had begun shifting funds to other advertising media five years ago. Twenty-nine percent said that they had not diverted their network television dollars into other media in 1987.

2. If your answer to the previous question was no, at what point would you seriously consider changing the media mix and allocating portions of your prime-time network TV budget to other media? When prime-time network audience share declines to:

70 percent

69 to 65 percent

64 to 60 percent

59 to 55 percent

54 to 50 percent

Below 50 percent

Wouldn't consider changing no matter how low

Of those who said that they had not modified their investment in network television advertising, 53 percent of the respondents said that they would seriously consider reallocating portions of their network television advertising budget to other media if the prime-time network television audience share declines to 65 percent, or would have reduced their network commitment before it reached that point; 26 percent said that they would react if it were to decline between 64 and 55 percent; and the remaining 21 percent said that they either would not react to the network television erosion issue until the audience share had shrunk below 50 percent, did not know, or could not make such a decision without knowing the relative advertising costs involved. None of the respondents in this group said that they would remain totally committed to advertising on network television regardless of how small its share of audience became.

3. If yes, which media (in ranking order) have benefited from the shift:

Cable TV

Independent TV stations

Radio

Newspapers

Outdoor

Direct response

Other

Of those who said that they had already reallocated advertising dollars previously committed to network television, 66 percent said that cable television has benefited most from the shift, 17 percent said that independent television stations or syndication (volunteered) were the prime beneficiaries, and the remainder were divided almost evenly among radio, sales promotion, magazines, and outdoor categories.

4. How much has the VCR contributed to prime-time network audience erosion?

Significantly

Somewhat

Very little

Not at all

Twelve percent of all respondents felt that the videocassette recorder had significantly contributed to prime-time network television audience decline, 63 percent said that the videocassette recorder was somewhat responsible for network audience erosion, and 25 percent felt that the videocassette recorder had had very little effect on the problem of audience erosion. None of the respondents stated that network television erosion had been unaffected by the videocassette recorder.

5. How do you perceive each of the following network TV viewing behaviors has affected your company's TV advertising effectiveness in prime time?

Watching rented or purchased videos in prime time
Significantly
Somewhat
Very little
Not at all

Time-shifting (taping from other dayparts for playback in prime time)
Significantly
Somewhat
Very little
Not at all

Flipping or zapping (changing channels to avoid commercials)
Significantly
Somewhat

Very little

Not at all

Zipping (fast-forwarding through commercials in taped programs)

Significantly

Somewhat

Very little

Not at all

In order of magnitude of negative effect (on network television viewing behavior): Sixty-nine percent of the respondents perceived that
flipping or zapping (changing channels to avoid commercials) had
either significantly or somewhat affected their companies' television
advertising effectiveness in prime time. Sixty-three percent perceived
that the watching of prerecorded videotapes (rented or purchased)
in prime time had either significantly or somewhat affected their companies' television advertising effectiveness. Fifty-three percent of the
respondents perceived that the practice of zipping (fast-forwarding
through commercials in taped programs) had either significantly or
somewhat affected their companies' television advertising effectiveness. Thirty-nine percent perceived that time-shifting (taping from other
dayparts for playback in prime time) had either significantly or somewhat affected their companies' television advertising effectiveness.

SUMMARY

The national television advertiser community has gone through
three major stages of development since it was born in the late 1940s:
First, it quickly carried over to television the pattern of sponsor control and programing domination that had been the basis of advertisers' relationships with radio networks beginning in the early 1930s.
This period, which lasted until about 1959, was characterized by
single sponsorship of most network television programs and an important role in program development by sponsor's advertising
agencies.

Second, the national advertiser community started to relinquish
its control of programing after 1960, when television networks, encouraged by the federal government, asserted their determination to
prevent national advertisers from continuing to sponsor programs
individually or allowing their advertising agencies to conceive and
develop properties for network television. During this era, advertisers

began buying commercial availabilities in many different network shows rather than totally sponsoring programs. This trend reflected a new desire by advertisers to get more diverse exposure and greater, demographically targeted, efficiency for their advertising dollars.

Third, the national advertiser community started reducing the proportion of its total financial television commitment to the three major networks in the mid-1980s as advertisers began to pursue television audiences who were being lured away by such alternative electronic media delivery systems as cable television, videocassette recorders, and independent television stations. Advertisers' concerns were exacerbated by anxiety over rising network advertising costs, increasing commercial clutter, and fear that patterns of commercial avoidance ("zapping" and "zipping") were becoming endemic among their most desired target audiences. While television network revenues continue to grow at this time, the heads of all three television networks have expressed major concerns about their long-term prospects for remaining the premier mass medium in the United States.

5

The Nonbroadcast Videotape Market

The adoption of videotape and recording technology by the so-called "nonbroadcast market" took place shortly after the commercial introduction of the new medium in 1956 (nonbroadcast refers to the use of videotape by corporations, educational and medical institutions, religious organizations, the government (federal, state, and local), and the military).

The pattern of adoption of the technology by this market parallels to a large degree the developments in the technology itself—as the technology became more standardized and portable (i.e., accessible), the wider the adoption of videotape by the nonbroadcast market. The pattern of adoption can be seen readily from an analysis of (1) a review of the use of the medium as reported by users between 1959–1989, (2) interviews with veterans of the nonbroadcast television business (i.e., professionals who have been in the business from at least the early 1970s), and (3) various studies of the nonbroadcast market conducted between 1968 and 1987.

MARKET OVERVIEW

It has been over thirty-one years (as of this writing) since the first nonbroadcast user adopted videotape technology as a communications medium. And while in the late 1950s there was only a handful of users, today the numbers are much larger. According to *The Business of Nonbroadcast Television* (Stokes, 1988, p. 13), in 1987 the total number of nonbroadcast users was 49,000. This number was projected to reach 83,000 by 1995! (see Table 5.1). Percentage-wise, the business/industry (i.e., corporate) area represents the largest segment of the nonbroadcast market (see Table 5.2). Business/industry represents the largest segment of the nonbroadcast market not only in terms of number of users, but also with respect to dollars spent. According to the Knowledge Industry Publications (KIPI) study, *all* nonbroadcast users spent $5.5 billion in 1987. Of this total, $3.3 billion (or 60 percent) was spent by corporations. The study projected a total nonbroadcast market of $12.6 billion by 1995. (To put these figures in perspective, consider that movie box office receipts in 1989 were projected to be close to $5 billion, a sum already achieved by the nonbroadcast market in 1987!)

EARLY YEARS/EARLY USERS

There were a handful of videotape users in the noncommercial/nonbroadcast market in the early years, but their use of the medium set the pattern for future years. For example, on June 24, 1958, it was announced that the National Educational Television and Radio Center and its forty-three affiliated noncommercial television stations would be equipped gratis with videotape recorders and tape sufficient for thirty hours of programing on each recorder, plus a substantial amount for duplicating work at the center's facilities at Ann Arbor, Michigan. Delivery of both recorders and tape began in August.

Table 5.1
Nonbroadcast Television Users (number)

Type of Organization	# of Users 1987	# of Users 1995
Business/industry	23,000	40,000
Educational	11,000	19,000
Medical	8,000	13,000
Government	5,000	7,000
Nonprofit	2,000	4,000
Total	49,000	83,000

Source: J.T. Stokes, *The business of nonbroadcast television '88*, Knowledge Industry Publications, (1988). Reprinted with permission of Knowledge Industry Publications.

Table 5.2
Nonbroadcast Television Users (percent)

Type of Organization	% of Market
Business/Industry	46.9
Educational	22.5
Medical	16.3
Government	10.2
Nonprofit	4.1

Source: J.T. Stokes, *The business of nonbroadcast television '88*, Knowledge Industry Publications, (1988). Reprinted with permission of Knowledge Industry Publications.

Making all this possible was a Ford Foundation grant of $2,706,000 for the recorders, and a 3M grant of $750,000 for tape (*The Changing Picture*, 1959, p. 45).

In the fall of 1958, the U.S. Air Force previewed videotape with "the expressed purpose of 'sparking staff imagination on possible uses'," such as in research and development in danger areas and staff briefings. A few weeks later it was announced "videotape . . . is . . . being adapted by branches of the armed services . . . for various types of research tests where immediate playback of picture is required".

The first installation of videotape technology in the U.S. nonbroadcast "educational" market was at the University of Texas, Austin, in November 1958. At the time, the university planned to use tape both for closed-circuit teaching and the distribution of programs to commercial stations. R. F. Schenkkan and N. W. Willett, director and technical supervisor, respectively, of the university's radio-television system, cited flexibility of scheduling classes, increase in studio flexibility, multiple reruns, easy and economical erasure, self-criticism, program building over a long period, sharing, and saving of production time as reasons for the adoption of the medium (p. 44).

The first reported use of the medium in the nonbroadcast "corporate" context occurred in January 1959 when Buick videotaped a roundtable discussion among some of its star salespeople. A major reason for the use of the medium given was videotape's "flexibility" (p. 51).

Even though the corporate segment of the nonbroadcast market does not represent the entire market, it is nonetheless the largest segment, both in terms of users and dollars spent. And while "programing" in the corporate context is not exactly the same as programing in educational, governmental, military, medical, and religious organizations, it is safe to say that the adoption of videotape technology for corporate television programing fairly represents the adoption of the medium by the nonbroadcast market as a whole. Thus, we will examine the corporate market segment as a means of developing an overview of the total nonbroadcast market.

CORPORATE NETWORK PROGRAMING

Nonbroadcast programing can be divided into seven broad categories: sales training, skills training, role playing, sales promotion/marketing, employee communications, employee news, and external communications. The use of videotape in the corporate context is first reported in 1959, three years after the commercial broadcast introduction of the medium. Six out of the seven programing applications were first reported *before* 1971. From the pattern of use reported in Table 5.3 one can see that the first four categories represent applications not requiring wide distribution to decentralized audiences—sales training, sales/marketing, skill training and role playing are applications in which the audience is highly specific and may or may not be decentralized (i.e., with respect to the origination point of the programming). On the other hand, employee communications, employee news, and external communications represent programing that is by definition inherently distributed to decentralized audiences.

Table 5.3
Nonbroadcast Video Applications: First Reports

Category/Application	First Report
Sales training	1959 (January)
Sales promotion/marketing	1959 (February)
Skill training	1960
Role playing	1964
Employee communications	1967
Employee news	1970
External communications	1980

As we shall see, and as the technology chapter has already laid the foundation for, as the videotape technology became more accessible (i.e., more standardized and portable), the more widely corporate television programing was distributed to decentralized audiences.

THE LATE 1950s–LATE 1960s: SALES AND SKILLS TRAINING

Sales Training . . . Electrovisually

It is fitting that sales training is the earliest reported nonbroadcast application of videotape in the corporate context. After all, America is a country based on entrepreneurial spirit and business enterprise. The use of the videotape medium by corporate America is, therefore, but one more example of America's businessmen's adoption of technology to advance economic motives.

The October 1959 edition of *The Changing Picture in Video Tape for 1959–1960*, published by 3M, reports that the Buick organization used videotape as part of a thirty-one city closed-circuit television session for Buick dealer salesmen in January 1959. Since this is essentially the *first* reported use of the medium in the corporate context, it is worth noting:

> From the thousands of men who sell Buicks across the country the company selected four for its telecast meeting. These were members of Buick Royal Purple Salesmasters, the elite of dealership salesmen.
>
> They became a panel, interviewed on the telecast to elicit the secrets of their selling. They also served as a sounding board for ideas put forth by other salesmen who were picked up by remote camera crews right in the actual dealer showrooms.
>
> A big aid to relaxing the cast—and unknown to the audience —was the pretaping of the entire program the day before the meeting. Because it was put on tape a day before, salesmen on the panel didn't have to worry about mistakes. If the show didn't go right, it could be done again. This insurance was a psychological tranquilizer. It was unnecessary to retape the program or to put it on live the next day (as was planned originally).
>
> . . . Images on a big screen were as clear as live transmission. . . . Flexibility of tape, plus the insurance factor, almost demand prerecording for performances by non-professionals. . . . With possibilities of slip-ups when you use remote pickups, as with the Buick telecast, tape is a director's dream.

If a remote doesn't come through properly, it can be picked up later and the tape spliced where it belongs. (p. 51).

Electronic Selling

On February 3, 1959, the Ford Tractor and Implement Division of the Ford Motor Company (Dearborn, Michigan) used videotape as part of its marketing effort to demonstrate equipment on closed-circuit television for farm equipment dealers. The demonstrations were made possible by the advent of the first completely self-contained mobile video unit built by Ampex for an estimated cost of $185,000. The closed-circuit presentation originated out of NBC's studios in Hollywood, California. The use of the mobile unit represented only the second time the unit had been employed (p. 17).

A major reason for the use of the videotape medium was the "instant playback" feature. The farm equipment had been videotaped in operation in Yuma, Arizona. Had film been used and a sequence failed to turn out properly, the entire operation would have had to have been repeated a day or two later. The videotape medium allowed production personnel to play back shots instantly and reshoot immediately (p. 17).

Another early use of videotape for sales promotion and marketing purposes took place July 16–19, 1959, at the Industrial Finishing Exposition at the Detroit Artillery Armory. The user was the Udylite Corporation of Warren, Michigan. The company furnished its exposition booth with soft chairs and a theater-size TV screen to run a continuous showing of a half-hour plant tour televised by closed circuit. After the tour, booth visitors were invited to personally visit the plant where a hospitality center was maintained during the exposition. According to then Advertising Director Robert C. Trees, Udylite chose videotape instead of live closed-circuit because it was able to "present scenes from every corner of the sprawling factory and research center in a tight continuity—at a fraction the cost and time that the same continuity on film would require—and with picture quality indistinguishable from live TV" (p. 57).

The Ubiquitous Instructor

Videotape for skill training in the corporate context was first reported in 1960. Continuing its tradition of leadership in this area, the company reporting the use of the medium for the education of its own employees was 3M.

It was Tuesday. The time was shortly before 4:30 in the afternoon. Groups of employees began to congregate at six locations throughout their company where television receiving sets had been set up. The employees were armed with pencils, papers, and workbooks as they settled themselves in before the monitors.

Sharply at 4:30, the television beamed in clear with the sound of the announcer's voice identifying himself. He went on to inform the viewers that they were watching Channel 2, St. Paul/Minneapolis, the educational channel of the Twin Cities area. The program they were about to see was the first of a twelve-week video-taped course in "Efficient reading." ("New Channel," 1960, pp. 8–9)

The Electrovisual Mirror

The first report of videotape's use as a role playing tool appears in the January 1966 issue of *Training in Business and Industry*. In the article, the author states, "The Institute—GM's central training agency—initiated television playback in the fall of 1964" (Carter, 1966, p. 38). Thus the earliest reported use of videotape for role playing purposes apparently occurred some eight years after the introduction of commercially viable videotape and magnetic recording technology.

Role playing can be defined as a training environment in which two or more trainees are placed in a simulated situation in which each plays a predefined role. The most obvious example is in sales training. One example might be as follows: the product to be sold is life insurance. In the role playing situation, the physical environment is a couple's home. One salesperson might play the role of the husband, another trainee, the role of the salesperson. Videotape's role in this context is to instantly record the interaction among the players and provide an instant mirror of the trainees' performance following the role play.

The 1969 Stroh Study

A 1969 study published by the American Management Association (AMA) gives some summary and insight into the technological state-of-the-art of videotape's use in the corporate context during the 1960s. For example, in the foreword, John W. Enell, vice president of research for the AMA states:

While video tape recording has been commercially viable for about ten years, early equipment was large, nonportable and very expensive. A steady stream of technical developments in fields such as solid state research and microcircuitry has cut away these obstacles. Current videotape equipment is compact, portable and reasonably priced. These sharply improved qualities have opened the way to scores of possible applications. (Stroh, 1969, p. 5)

In his introduction, though, the study's author, Stroh, points to the conflicts the new medium was placing on corporate management.

Members of top management and personnel management who select and train people and who guide management development activities are currently being deluged with contradictory articles about videotape recording. Proponents claim that the uses and effectiveness of this new equipment offer a panacea for development ills. Conversely, antagonists counter that videotape recording is just another fad that will pass or that its misuse may cause devastating and permanent psychological damage to trainees. (p. 9)

Stroh counters with a critique of videotape equipment manufacturers.

Many recorders will not play back tapes on another machine—even one that was manufactured by the same company. There are no industry standards for basics, such as the number of lines of picture resolution, the number of recording heads, the speed of the tape over the recording heads, and tape width. In addition, there are serious problems with equipment servicing and few facilities for training new users in the field. (pp. 9–10)

Despite these technological problems, users, according to the AMA study, found value in the new medium. The feature considered essential by the greatest number of participants (68 percent) was rapid forward and reverse. The next most essential feature, reported by 51 percent of the participants, was playback on other machines.

Of the 109 companies reported having VTR equipment, 72 percent stated their major use was for sales training (p. 78). One of the most prevalent applications was role playing, for example, a trainee was confronted with a selling situation involving a customer. Stroh reports that after the role playing, the trainee was shown a playback of the performance and simultaneously given an oral critique (p. 16).

Eighty-nine percent of users reported they believed the cost of their equipment was justified; only 5 percent emphatically stated, "Not justified yet"; and 6 percent answered "Not sure."

THE 1970s: CORPORATE NETWORKS ARE BORN

While the late 1950s to late 1960s can be characterized as a period during which corporate managements used videotape in a highly centralized fashion (for sales training, skill training, role playing at company headquarters or centralized/regional training areas), the 1970s can be described as the period in which corporate America spawned its equivalent of the "television (albeit nonbroadcast) network." This phenomenon was as a direct result of developments in videotape technology.

Two studies of the corporate television industry in the 1970s not only reflect these technological developments but also the impact of the technology on nonbroadcast programing applications and distribution systems.

While the 1969 Stroh study is the first extant overview of the corporate video industry, it contrasts sharply with *Private Television Communications: A Report to Management* (Brush & Brush, 1974), published by KIPI, which claimed to "establish for the first time the true dimensions of the rapidly expanding field of private and industrial television" (p. 5).

Issues of technology standardization and portability, similar to those found in the 1969 Stroh study, crop up in this report as well. For example, the authors state:

> One of the confusing things about private television has been the large number of formats available and the so-called lack of standardization. . . . This means that a tape made on a one-inch VTR of one manufacturer can only be played on one of that manufacturer's machines. All one-half-inch, open reel VTR's imported since 1970 can accept tapes made on any other similar EIAJ machine.
>
> As of now, all three-quarter-inch videocassettes are fully interchangeable and there is no problem between machines of different manufacturers since they are all made under the same Sony license. (pp. 72–73)

With respect to production equipment, the authors note there are basically two kinds: portable and studio equipment. Portable equipment accounts for most of the production origination equipment in the private television industry in terms of "number of units in use" (p. 74). Further, "most portable equipment is in the one-half-inch (EIAJ) open reel format (mostly black and white), although the three-quarter-inch U-Matic was considered portable by a lot of users. On the other hand, studio equipment, while usually more expensive and technically superior was considered a lot less portable" (p. 75).

Even though there are five years between the 1969 Stroh and the 1974 KIPI study, the latter report reflects that sales training in particular and training in general were still major uses of the videotape medium.

The growth of the medium, in the corporate context at least, can be seen in the number of programs being produced—apparently at an average number of twenty-seven per year (per organization).

The number of viewing locations is also a major difference between the two studies. The former study did not even cover this area; the 1974 KIPI study does. Clearly, the commercial introduction of the three-quarter-inch videocassette in 1971 created an efficient and effective means of creating corporate television networks.

The discussion on distribution systems is what perhaps singularly distinguishes the context of the 1969 Stroh study from the 1974 KIPI study. For example, in the latter study the authors state, "It is probably safe to say that following the determination of the message . . . the next most important element in private television is how the material is going to be distributed" (p. 79). Without the presence of the "standardized" three-quarter-inch videocassette, this statement probably would not have been made (let alone the entire 1974 study).

The second 1970s study of the corporate television industry was published in 1977 by the International Television Association (ITVA; then known as the International Industrial Television Association). This study also focused on technological aspects. According to the authors:

> Decentralization of video production is one of the major trends. . . . In 1976 three-quarters of the respondents having in-house facilities shot some or all of their programs outside the studio. These users produced an average of 39 percent of their programs on location. Almost one-third shot more than 61 percent of their programs in the field. (Brush & Brush, 1977, p. 55)

The authors make the connection between the technological innovation of the time and this trend.

> The ENG [electronic newsgathering] revolution began at the 1975 National Association of Broadcasters convention with the coming together of . . . the time-base-corrector (which had been introduced at NAB two years earlier), the portable Sony three-quarter-inch videocassette recorder (new that year), and the three tube Plumbicon portable color camera . . . corporate video producers quickly climbed aboard the ENG bandwagon. (p. 57)

This study also surveyed the use of the medium and found "Specific Job Training" to be the top ranked application. Once again training was the dominant use of the medium with management communications, safety, direct sales, and security analyst presentations moving up a notch or two.

The broadening use of the videotape medium in the mid-1970s is reflected in the broadening number of programs being produced by corporations. While the 1974 study accounted for numbers of programs "over 50," the 1976 study accounted for numbers of programs "over 100".

The growth in the number of viewing locations was also evidence of the medium's growth. In 1974, the percentage of companies with only one location was 14 percent; this had dropped to 6.8 percent by 1977. In the former year the percentage of companies with twenty-one or more locations was thirty-six percent, compared to forty-five percent in 1977. And while the 1974 study apparently did not deliberately attempt to specifically measure the percentage of companies with locations with over fifty viewing locations, the 25.5 percent that shows up in the 1977 report is a strong indication of growth (p. 71).

Over nineteen percent of the total had viewing locations between fifty-one and 200, 5 percent had viewing locations numbering between 201 and 999, and about 1 percent had over 999 viewing locations. According to the 1977 study, the leading form of distribution (75.2 percent of respondents) was the three-quarter-inch videocassette (p. 71).

Another major difference between the 1974 and 1977 reports is the observation users were distributing programs to overseas locations in the latter year. According to the report, 23.6 percent of 225 respondents were distributing programs overseas (p. 79).

Top Management Gets Visible

The shift of the medium from a centralized audience setting in the 1950s–1960s to decentralized audience distribution in the 1970s is clearly in evidence in the "employee communications" programing category. Again, developments in the technology give support for the shift.

The General Employee Communications programing application covers a broad area and includes: policy announcements, changes in top management, benefits information, retirement information, and orientation programing.

From the available evidence, it is clear top management became very visible via videotape in the 1970s. In fact, the evidence indicates top executives were not only a part of these kinds of videos but were also the "stars." This use of the medium seems to have satisfied a desire on the part of management to reach all employees, not only at headquarters, but also in field locations in a short period of time after the creation of the program. This application also indicated a "production style" break from typically highly structured training programs: many of the events videotaped were structured in some way but not highly scripted.

Even though the employee communications application receives industry attention in the 1970s and the advent of the three-quarter-inch U-matic videocassette gives rise to corporate networks (which, in turn, fosters the growth of employee communications via videotape), the first reported use of the videotape medium for employee communications appears in an August 1970 *Education Television* article (now *Educational and Industrial Television*). Author Lu Bartlow (1970), then public relations supervisor for Illinois Bell, writes: "The first major information program management presentation dealing with special employment projects for the disadvantaged—was videotaped in September 1967" (p. 18).

Clearly, the use of videotape for employee communications is in evidence in the late 1960s, but it is the advent of a standardized distribution medium (the three-quarter-inch videocassette) which enables management to, in effect, decentralize its communications efforts to all employees. The use of the medium for news is similar in pattern.

The Electrovisual House Organ

The earliest reported use of videotape for employee news is Smith Kline and French's (Philadelphia) news show, started in 1970. Curiously, the 1974 KIPI study does not have a category for employee news. The 1977 ITVA study, however, does and ranks employee news as ninth highest, as does the 1979 Knowledge Industry study (a 1980 ITVA study ranks the category as sixteenth highest—out of twenty categories).

Employee news via videotape, according to the available evidence, seems to have enjoyed a period of considerable popularity. The reported activities of persons and corporations engaged in employee news seem to corroborate the studies' findings. No other use of videotape for corporate communications purposes attracted as much attention from the consumer and trade press in the 1970s as employee news. For example, the March 19, 1973, *ETV Newsletter* reported "Smith Kline & French to Run Seminars on How It Uses CCTV for Employee Communications" (p. 4). In the June 11, 1973, issue of the same publication it was announced Chase Manhattan Bank would host the second annual one-day conference of "corporate television house organ producers" ("Chase Manhattan Bank," 1973, p. 3). The *Videoplay Report* (1973, pp. 1–4) later reported thirty-eight video producers from nineteen companies attended, including such companies as Chase Manhattan Bank, Con Edison, Citibank, Dupont, Equitable Life, Smith Kline, AT&T, Aetna Life and Casualty, and Western Electric. A third annual conference was scheduled for 1974 but was never held ("Employee News Video Conference," 1974, p. 4).

Corporate employee news via videotape attracted the attention of the business press in the mid-1970s when the *Wall Street Journal* published an article entitled, "Some Firms Like It if Their Employees Watch TV at Work" (Morganthaler, 1974, pp. 1, 22). Various company news shows were described and analyzed, including Bethlehem Steel, New England Mutual Life, Citibank, Smith Kline, Metropolitan Life, and AT&T. According to the article, news shows varied from daily (such as AT&T's *Monitor* program shown at a headquarters location) to Bethlehem Steel's *Nine Minutes* program (reportedly sent to thirty-eight offices and plants on videocassettes).

Employee news made the big time, so to speak, when an article appeared in an October 1975 issue of *TV Guide*. Entitled "But First, This Flu Shot Reminder" (Hall, 1975) the article reported that an estimated forty major corporations "produce a regularly scheduled employee TV news show" (pp. 24–25). *Business Week* got into the act with a March 14, 1977, article entitled "TV That Competes with the Office Grapevine." In it, companies such as Ashland Oil, Exxon, Travelers Insurance, Bell Telephone of Pennsylvania, and John Hancock Mutual Life are mentioned (pp. 49, 51, 54).

The special interest in employee news was reflected in a *Corporate Television News Survey* (1978) conducted in August/September 1978 by a special committee of the ITVA. It was an attempt to gather general data on viewership. The survey aimed to find out the history of the television news program, its method of distribution, and the program format. Twenty companies participated in the survey.

The findings showed 80 percent of the respondents had a television news program. Almost two-thirds reported they had been producing an employee news show for more than a year. Fifty percent indicated a program frequency of weekly to biweekly. About a third reported a monthly program frequency, with the balance showing the program on a quarterly basis.

Finally, as if the TV employee news phenomenon had come full circle, Tom Thompson (1980) (producer of the longest running TV employee news show in the United States—Smith Kline's *TV News*) wrote a book entitled *Organization TV News*. In it Thompson describes in much detail the whys and wherefores of the program—the entire process for producing an employee news show on video.

Closing Out the 1970s

KIPI (which had published a 1974 study) conducted a survey of the nonbroadcast video industry in 1979 (published in 1980). The findings of this survey showed the nonbroadcast market (all segments) had grown dramatically during the 1970s (see Table 5.4).

According to the survey, in 1979, there were 27,000 nonbroadcast users in the United States.

In 1973 the ITVA held its first conference in Washington, D.C. ITVA membership was then 300 organizations. Compare this to the 13,500 organizations in the business/industry category just seven years later!

THE 1980s: REACHING OUT

One could describe the 1980s as the decade when not only corporations, but other nonbroadcast organizations reached out and touched everyone with videotape technology based messages.

The external communications application is the use of videotape for community relations, investor relations, public affairs, public service announcements, and government relations.

A survey of the nonbroadcast corporate video industry (*Private Television Communications: Into the Eighties*, Brush & Brush, 1981) was conducted in 1980 by the ITVA. The paucity of reported use of videotape for external communications in both the trade and consumer press is echoed in this ITVA study (see Table 5.5). For example, the report's authors reference four areas of external communications

Table 5.4
Nonbroadcast Video, 1979

TYPE OF ORGANIZATION	NUMBER OF USERS
Business/Industry	13,500
Education	5,000
Medical	5,000
Government	3,000
Nonprofit	800
TOTAL	27,000

Source: R. Dranov, L. Moore & A. Hickey, *Video in the '80s,* White Plains, NY: Knowledge Industry Publications, (1980), p. 13. Reprinted with permission of Knowledge Industry Publications.

Table 5.5
External Applications, 1980

Application	Ranking
Community/public relations	13
Shareholder information	15
Labor/government relations	19
Security analysts presentations	20

Source: J. Brush and D. Brush. *Private television communications: Into the eighties (the third Brush report)*, New Providence: International Television Association, (1981). Distributed by HI Press, Inc. Reprinted with permission of HI Press.

with the indicated "low" rank order. However, this trend was to change by the latter part of the decade.

In the 1981 ITVA study a user was defined as an organization that has more than one playback location, or that produces its own programs and/or has its own studio (Brush & Brush, 1981, p. 12). Significantly, by the early 1980s about 53 percent of all business/industry respondents reported having networks between one and twenty-five locations; nearly 16 percent had more than 100 locations.

The use of the medium was again surveyed. The results were fairly consistent with earlier studies: "training" was still one of the major and dominant uses of the medium. However, there were some shifts.

Specific job training (which received the highest percentage in 1977) had slipped to second position. Basic skill training, ranked third in the 1977 survey, was now top of the list. Perhaps more significantly, management development (ranked second in the 1977 survey) was now ranked seventh. Taking third position was employee orientation, a category that did not even appear in the 1977 survey.

Several categories had been added to the list, specifically, economic information and labor/government relations. This reflected, according to the authors, the greater diversity of programing being produced in 1980 as compared to 1976.

The 1981 survey also researched the volume of video programs. The authors point out that the median number of programs produced in 1976 was 20.8. In 1980, the number was 18, an apparent drop of 13 percent. The authors surmised the decrease was because users "are opting for a higher quality of product for their in-house clients rather than grinding out an ever-increasing number of programs each year. . . . There is a greater tendency to use video for only the applications and the internal needs for which it is best suited" (p. 60).

The study points out that in 1973 the median number of viewing locations was 8. In 1976 that number had jumped to 18. In 1980 the median number of viewing locations was 34, an over four-fold increase in seven years (p. 82).

The means of distributing programming was also tracked in the 1980 survey (see Table 5.6).

The ITVA also published *Private Television Communications: The New Directions* (Brush & Brush, 1986), which gave further indications of the medium's continued adoption by corporate organizations.

The 1986 ITVA study indicates that between 1980 and 1985 training continued in the top ten. Further, between the two years, in terms of applications, not much movement seems to have occurred among the categories.

Table 5.6
Primary Means of Distribution (N = 323)

MEANS OF DISTRIBUTION	% OF TOTAL
3/4 inch videocassette	53.3
1/2 inch VHS videocassette	13.3
1/2 inch Beta videocassette	11.8
3/4 inch and VHS	5.9
3/4 inch and other medium	4.3
3/4 inch and film	3.7
3/4 inch and Beta	2.2
Other videotape formats	
(cartridge, open reel)	1.5
16mm and 8mm film	1.5
Cable TV	0.3

Source: J. Brush and D. Brush. *Private television communications: Into the eighties (the third Brush report)*, New Providence: International Television Association, (1981). Distributed by HI Press, Inc. Reprinted with permission of HI Press.

Paralleling the growth of video networks, the number of programs produced, according to the 1986 ITVA study, had also increased compared to 1980 figures. Level of programing had shifted since 1980 at both ends of the spectrum. Fewer organizations were producing ten or less programs a year. In 1980 thirty percent of the respondents fell into that range, while in 1985 only eighteen percent produced less than ten programs a year, a decrease of thirty-nine percent. At the other end of the scale, the study found that while 16.6 percent of the respondents produced sixty-one or more programs a year in 1980, nineteen percent produced that number in 1985, an increase of nearly 15 percent.

The most startling difference between the 1980 and 1985 ITVA studies is the size of video networks in terms of number of viewing locations.

In the former study the largest video network size was "over fifty". According to the latter study, 57.7 percent of the sample (N = 227) reported viewing locations of fifty-one or more, with the largest number of locations at "over 1,000," a further indication of the growth of corporate networks started in the 1970s. Further, program distribution to overseas locations had increased. Almost one-third, 31.2 percent of the respondents distributed programing internationally, compared to 23.6 percent in the 1977 survey.

The impact of the VHS and Beta half-inch videotape formats are clearly in evidence in the 1986 ITVA study with respect to programing distribution (see Table 5.7). The three-quarter-inch videocassette as the primary means of distribution fell to a level of just 32.2 percent from a high in 1980 of 53.3 percent, a decrease of 40 percent, with the half-inch VHS format at the 54.6 percent level—virtually a trading of places in five years.

Table 5.7
Means of Distribution, 1980/1986

	% of total	
Means of distribution	1980	1986
1/2-inch VHS videocassettes	13.3	54.6
3/4-inch videocassettes	53.3	32.2
1/2-inch Beta videocassettes	11.8	11.6

Source: J. Brush and D. Brush, *Private television communications: The new directions (the fourth Brush report)*, New York: HI Press, Inc., (1986). Reprinted with permission of HI Press.

These findings are consistent with prior technological developments. As the videotape medium has become smaller in format and less expensive, the primary means of distribution in the corporate context has followed suit.

Hi Press Inc. published *Private Television Communications/Update '88* (Brush & Brush, 1988) as an update to the 1986 ITVA study in response to not technological changes per se, but changes in America's corporate topography, that is, "the effects that the current wave of mergers, acquisitions, takeovers, reorganizations and downsizings are having on corporate television" (p. 3). Of the several effects, the authors mention that corporate television departments had increasingly become full-charge back operations (contributing to the bottom line), independent profit centers (in some cases), divested into independent production companies, or cutback.

This study reflects the continuing growth of distribution networks as indicated by number of viewing locations. Table 5.8 reflects the virtual geometric growth.

The authors observe that hybrid networks continue to be common, with one-half-inch and three-quarter-inch continuing to be the dominant distribution media (see Table 5.9). But the figures also indicate that satellites and in-house closed-circuit and master antenna television (CCTV and MATV) systems are gaining in momentum.

This survey indicated that for the first time an almost thirty-year trend was in the process of being reversed. While training has been the mainstay of corporate television programing, it appeared that general employee communications and certain external communications

Table 5.8
Median Number of Viewing Locations

MEDIAN NUMBER OF VIEWING LOCATIONS

1973	8
1977	18
1981	34
1985	70
1988	113

Source: J. Brush and D. Brush, *Private television communications: The fourth Brush report, update '88*, La Grangeville, NY: HI Press, Inc., (1988). Reprinted with permission of HI Press.

Table 5.9
Program Distribution

Means of Distribution	% of Total
1/2-inch VHS	96.0
3/4-inch videocassette	73.7
1/2-inch Beta	28.3
In-house CCTV and MATV	19.2
Satellite	16.2
Videodisc	8.1
8mm videotape	5.1
Microwave	5.1
Other (including film)	2.0

Source: J. Brush and D. Brush, *Private television communications: The fourth Brush report, update '88*, La Grangeville, NY: HI Press, Inc., (1988). Reprinted with permission of HI Press.

programing applications were becoming more dominant. As the authors put it: "In the past, training applications usually paid the freight and [general] communications went along for the ride. The ranking[s] . . . show that this situation is now becoming reversed" (p. 6).

Generally speaking, the authors posit, "we see more and more video programing being aimed at outside audiences such as customers, community groups, and the general public." Further, "We are seeing just the beginning of a significant impact of corporate communications reaching into every area of our lives with the stories of products and services, community impact statements, stockholders information, and employee communications becoming as commonplace as the broadcast Evening News and the tape we rent on a weekend to entertain the kids" (p. 8).

MOVING INTO THE 1990s

To gain a perspective on the use of the videotape medium in the corporate context in the late 1980s and its prospects for the 1990s, four corporate video managers were interviewed in depth. The managers were selected because (1) their experience covered fifteen to twenty years of developments in the corporate video industry, (2) each represented a different section of the country, and (3) each represented a different kind of industry. The individuals interviewed were:

Jeannie E. Tasker, director of televideo services, National Advanced Systems, Santa Clara, California. Since 1985, Ms. Tasker has managed a six-person staff, producing approximately seventy-five programs a year for National Advanced Systems, National Semiconductor (the parent company), and Datachecker Systems (another subsidiary) in the areas of marketing, training, and employee communications. A nineteen-year veteran of the corporate television industry, Ms. Tasker started her career as a producer/director/writer with Pacific Bell. After nine years with Pacific Bell, she became a consultant and manager of media services for the Amdahl Corporation. She has served twice as national vice president of the International Television Association, on the ITVA's International-Program Committee, and various positions with the ITVA's San Francisco Chapter. She received a bachelor's degree in radio television from Humboldt State University, Eureka, California, in 1968.

Al Bond is a consultant in satellite conferencing for numerous organizations, including Texas Instruments (Dallas, Texas), LTV, Mary Kay Cosmetics, Southland Corporation, Pizza Hut, The Children's Television Workshop, and the International Television Association. Mr. Bond joined Texas Instruments in 1968 after an assignment with the Manned Space Craft Center in Houston where he worked as liaison with the radio and television networks throughout the Gemini program and into the Apollo series. Mr. Bond is past president of the International Television Association and a former member of the Board of Directors. He holds the distinction of being the only two-term chairman of the board of the ITVA. He is chairman of the advisory committee of the Radio/Television/Film Department of North Texas State University and a member of the advisory committee of the Dallas Independent School District Television Education Program. He is listed in Videography's *Who's Who in Corporate Television* for the years 1977–1981 and 1985. He received a BFA in Radio/Television Production from the University of Texas in 1961.

Stephen Mulligan is director of audio visual communications for Allstate Insurance Company, Northbrook, Illinois. He has had fifteen years experience managing internal communications and corporate television functions. He pioneered the use of television for employee communications at Allstate, installing the INTERCOM video communications network in 140 locations across the country. He currently manages the Audio Visual facility for Allstate, which includes a staff of thirty professionals and over $3 million of equipment. The facility annually produces over 200 programs in film, video, multimedia, and audio cassette. Mulligan is chairman of the board of the International Television Association, the association of over 9,000 video professionals worldwide. He served two years as ITVA treasurer and is a past international president. Mr. Mulligan was also chair of the Electronic Communications Council for the International Association of Business Communicators. He has lectured at NYU, Northwestern University, Indiana University, and Columbia College on the subject of corporate video. Mulligan earned a Bachelor of Journalism from the University of Missouri, Columbia, and a Master of Science in Management from Lake Forest School of Management.

Grant Williams is an independent writer and director of corporate television programing with a background that extends to 1971. While in the U.S. Army, he served as senior director for the Armed Forces Network in Germany. Following a brief stint in commercial and news production at an NBC affiliate in Oregon, Mr. Williams was hired by Georgia Pacific Corporation to pioneer the company's use of video communications. For nearly ten years, he managed the design and use of video for internal communications and training, expanding the company's video network to over 300 national and international locations. His current clients include Georgia Pacific, Burlington Industries, Coca-Cola, Hardee's Food Systems, Coopers & Lybrand, BellSouth, and C&S National Bank. Williams has authored "Between Takes" since 1981 for *Video Manager* and has been a featured speaker for various professional organizations.

The Interviews

The four in-depth interviews with Ms. Tasker and Mssrs. Bond, Mulligan, and Williams reflected an "external" perspective and a broadness of application consistent with the trends noted in the early and mid-1980s.

Question 1: What, in your view, are the major technology developments of the 1980s?

Jeannie Tasker, interview, October 28, 1987: Definitely the Betacam. It's made television production more portable. There's less studio footage; programs are less studio oriented. The home market has also had an influence. I'm talking about the VHS. We're now able to produce programing for employees to take home.

The VHS has made a big difference in terms of distribution. Computerized graphics is another example. Low priced digital video effects devices used in post-production.

Interactive video disc is still being talked about, particularly by our training people, particularly when linked with computer based training. There is computer based training. But interactive video disc, there's not much of it.

Teleconferencing has really come into its own. There's a lot of ad hoc going on and private networks. A lot of training is being brought in by satellite.

Al Bond, interview October 28, 1987: Satellite communications is most available today as a distribution and interactive medium. We can now reach audiences at home; people can view a program there at their leisure.

Camera technology certainly has taken a quantum leap in the last five years. Cameras are lighter; they produce a better picture and they're less expensive. And in terms of production technology I would say that the development of electronic graphics has certainly made a difference.

Steve Mulligan, interview, November 30, 1987: Basically, the technology is getting smaller, more portable, higher quality. Here I'm talking about camera technology and editing equipment. The half-inch broadcast formats are important. The development of digital effects equipment has also had an impact. I suppose interactive video disc is also important. But we're just getting into that.

Grant Williams, interview, December 7, 1987: Computer graphics for video, especially for animation. Another development is the Betacam one-half-inch technology. Computer graphics capabilities have substantially reduced the cost and time to do complex animation. The technology has become more accessible. You can use the technology to explain, visualize graphics. You can take the nonvisual and make it visual.

Question 2: What reasons do people give for the use of the videotape medium?

Tasker: There's greater acceptance of the need to communicate effectively internally. Senior management sees the need to communicate to employees. There's also a need to sell product, move more product. People see video as the most effective way. Typically a video is used in conjunction with something in print. Video works because it's live, it moves, you can now show it to the family. Video is so accepted. People don't read any more. Video provides a common message. Video is visually and aurally stimulating. And people can watch it at different times.

Bond: Why do people use the medium? The ability to communicate a consistent message. The consistent quality and reliability of hardware delivery systems. And the portability of distribution systems. They're smaller, lighter, and cheaper.

Mulligan: Consistency of the message is a major part of it. It's for this reason that we've been able to successfully sell video to management. With consistency, the information is not subject to interpretation. There's no reading between the lines. When a top executive presents a message in print it's one thing; when he gets into a video, it's another. The person is there in the flesh. It's real. Video has power. It can generate emotion through it. We're now doing programs that involve the telling of stories: about people. Allstate people talking about people, particularly extraordinary customer relations.

Williams: Cost. Ease of distribution. Video is becoming a universal format for corporate and home video. Speed of production. Relative ease of production versus film. It's a trusted medium. People say, "If it's on television, it must be so."

Question 3: How are other media influenced by videotape?

Tasker: There's more video being done even when print would do a better job. People just won't go through the manual. Print is being used as a reference. But people want to see the videotape. Video is being used more than multiscreen, because it's more portable. There's very little film being used at all. Not at all for distribution. Some stuff is shot on film but edited on videotape. Most people wouldn't know where to find a film projector.

Bond: Film is almost gone. And I mean 16mm film, except maybe high-speed film for production. Thirty-five millimeter slides is not necessarily growing. Multi-image still lives on. But the single projector slide show is almost gone. Most people are using video. There's no great leap forward for the interactive video disc. It costs too much. It's too complex. It's limited by hardware costs.

I see no massive change in use of print. It's more of an audiovisual support base. At press conferences we'll give away a video of a product as well as a print piece.

Mulligan: Everything is being driven by video. Video is the medium of the corporation. Even multi-image presentations are driven by videotape, technically speaking. Even executive speeches have some kind of video element as part of it. Communications is dominated by video.

We do perhaps one film a year. But we do about 230 videos a year. We have a close relationship with our print partners. Very often there'll be a print and video piece working together. They support each other. Slides are used for meeting support. The people who do the slides are not part of our department. They don't do a very good job of it. Video is so much easier to use.

Williams: In the area of graphics, computers were first used for producing slides. Nowadays, computer graphic devices are also being used to make graphics for video. The medium is being adapted for video. Also, these days die-hard film people are saying, "O.K. We'll shoot tape, too."

Question 4: What department is using videotape? Who is the audience? Where?

Tasker: Marketing is using it. And corporate communications is using it a lot more. It's being used especially if the company is a marketing type of company. More and more video is being used for external communications in addition to internal communications. Training is there always. But there's a lot more public service kinds of programs, to schools, community groups, and clubs.

Bond: There's more use of the medium. We're doing more with external audiences, customers and potential customers. For example, with a teleconference we gave recently on artificial intelligence, the feedback that we got was that the use of the teleconference medium allowed the technology to get out there years ahead. We're now able to reach audiences all over the world. We're reaching them in their offices, in the plant. We're coming to them. We can even access other company networks and plug into them. Internally, I see no change.

Mulligan: Can't think of one department that isn't using video. Even the accounting department is using video. Marketing and sales, of course.

Video programing is directed at very specific targeted audiences. Very few programs are seen by all employees. We have produced a couple of tapes directed at customers—consumer tips on how to make your home more secure—that are shown in claim offices. Next year we intend to produce videotapes for agents for use in customer homes on the VHS format.

Williams: Just about everyone is using video. It's universal. Departments throughout the organization. It's everywhere now. It touches everyone.

Question 5: What is the physical viewing environment?

Tasker: Because of the distribution capability, the home environment has become a place where videos are viewed. We've also built a customer theater in which video was part of the planning. Video is becoming part of the planned architecture. Video has also become a medium in conference rooms. Some companies are wiring their conference rooms. People just bring tapes to a meeting, along with their overhead foils and memos. Why has the overhead survived? Probably because it's quick and very cheap to produce. It's also informal.

Bond: Other than reaching external audiences in their offices and their plants, there's no real change. There are a few, perhaps, multimedia rooms that have been built with video integrated into them, but other than that, nothing else.

Mulligan: Tapes can be seen anywhere. At home, in little rooms all over the building. All over the place. We've made a deliberate attempt to make the video hardware more portable, so that people can move the equipment around all over the place and use it in any situation. The idea here is to make the viewing more portable, more flexible. No more people gathering in large groups. Someone can look at the tape at their convenience, anywhere.

Williams: You can find video in the classroom and in the home. That's a change, a relatively new development. There are now special teleconferencing rooms. Video setups in general assembly rooms. Conference rooms. Desk-top set-ups for customer presentations. Department stores on the floor, at the retail counter. At the convention booth, in the field on the back end of a truck. At military field headquarters.

Question 6: What do video professionals and users say about how the medium should be used?

Tasker: In the last five years there's been greater recognition that we're in the business of the company's business. Video is just one tool that we use to meet our company's needs. My producers love producing good creative programs. But they're not only concerned with the effectiveness of the program but also its creativeness. We have a broad perspective. We get involved in telecommunications, marketing plans, as well as video production. We're in the catbird seat. We ask what can the company be doing with video for marketing, training, corporate communications? Sometimes I think because we get involved with many departments, "My God, we ought to be running the company!" We also ask: Where do we belong in the company? Are we a service department or a communications function? The answer I think is yes to both. There are so many overlaps. Because of what we do, we get different groups together. I don't see the printing people having the same perspective. They say: this is the job; it will cost such and such; it will take so much time to do. People here tend to look beyond the day-to-day. People who are in this business look beyond every day. I think the technology has something to do with it.

Bond: We're a break-even entity. We're now at the corporate level. We support the entire corporation. So we have an overall perspective. Our problem is: What medium is most appropriate to solve each communications problem? In years past this wasn't so. We now have a bigger palate to draw from.

We're now involved in more real-time electronic communications. What we do now is a more integral part of product marketing. There's a younger management, moving up to senior management. I see us being a stronger arm of business in the future because the world is so visualized now.

Mulligan: More and more we're getting demands for top quality programs. Our clients are insisting on top quality. We just did a series of programs with an average cost of $50,000. Quality, even glitz, creates an image. Clients want sparkle and shine. We're even getting into original music scores. We're now expected to initiate programing ideas. As much as possible, when we go out on a shoot, after the shoot is over we attempt to find out what people want. Again, what people want is flexibility. They want convenience and independence in when and how they view the programing.

Williams: Used to be that a client would say, "Let's just tape a lecture." These days that kind of approach is no longer accepted. Clients want better production values. Another trend is that companies are going more and more to the outside to get programs done. They want the special effects and high end value but don't want to have to pay to have the equipment and personnel in house. Another trend is companies are allowing people to use their own home video cameras to record a lecture and setting up simple one-half-inch editing rooms for them to edit the material down. This way the small group of people that have a need for the content can have a video record of it at a low cost.

ANALYSIS

The interviewees' statements reflect the technological developments of the 1980s: camcorders, satellite teleconferencing, computer graphics, and the home video—VHS distribution capability. Issues of portability and accessibility (the factors that initiated the use of the videotape medium in 1959) are clearly in evidence. On the other hand, video disc technology, while mentioned, is not positioned in a highly positive tone.

The reasons for the use of the medium given by the interviewees reflect both technology and communications effectiveness issues. The interviewees mention video as a people medium, consistency of message and the technology, and the cost and the universal availability of the medium.

The interviewees comment that in the 1980s video is working even more with print as a communications partner—a trend evident in the 1956–1980 period. Also, 16mm is "almost gone," to use Al Bond's phrase. Other media, such as multi-image and graphics production, seem to be driven by video technology; that is, even computer graphics devices are being adapted to the video medium.

As McLuhan might have commented, by the late 1980s the videotape medium seems to be everywhere, used by all corporate departments for dissemination to a variety of internal and external audiences. And consistent with the findings from the 1956–1980 period, the medium is still being used, for the most part, to communicate with select audiences, rather than all employees or all external audiences. Also clear from (in particular) the interviewees' comments is that the medium is being used increasingly for reaching audiences external to the corporation.

The ubiquitous presence of the videotape medium in many physical locations is also reflected in the comments from interviewees. Videotape machines are seemingly in every environment, including the home. And there appears to be a conscious effort to make the medium as portable and accessible as possible from a distribution point of view.

With respect to working paradigms, the interviewees reflect two themes: (1) video professionals have a broad view of the corporation with respect to the use of the medium to help solve a variety of corporate communications problems; (2) an increased sensitivity to high production values. These corporate video managers reflect a broad perspective of the corporation as an entity, as compared to other media production functions, such as the print or slidemakers. And it appears that as the medium has become increasingly and universally accessible, video production managers and professionals report concern with higher production values, paralleling those of broadcast television.

These attitudes reflect the professional issues articulated by users in the 1956–1980 period, particularly after the 1971 commercial introduction of the three-quarter-inch videocassette. In effect, the comments of the interviewees regarding working paradigms are on the same continuum as reported by many other nonbroadcast video professionals working in the corporate context.

Even a cursory analysis of the various studies and reported uses of the videotape medium shows that a major expansion of the use of the medium in the nonbroadcast market occurred after 1971. Part of the evidence for this is the fact that virtually all the studies of the nonbroadcast use of videotape and most professional and consumer articles reporting use of the medium in the nonbroadcast context were published after 1971. Further, the International Television Association did not come into existence until after 1971.

What occurred in 1971? In 1971 Sony began to commercially market the three-quarter-inch U-Matic videocassette. In technological terms, in 1971 videotape truly became accessible: one three-quarter-inch videocassette could fit a Sony machine, or one made by a variety of other manufacturers. The videocassette also eliminated the mechanical (i.e., user) problems associated with one-inch and one-half-inch reel-to-reel helical scan (the precursor to the videocassette) and the bulkiness of the original two-inch wideband videotape form (until a few years ago the standard in broadcast television).

In diffusion of technology terms, the advent of the three-quarter-inch U-Matic videocassette resulted in a significant increase in the number of adopters (both senders and receivers). The number of adopters grew because the technology became more accessible. Harold Innis would probably have pointed out that videotape, particularly in the videocassette form, was a light, highly portable and transportable medium. And given this definition, videotape was a medium with a bias toward space—the medium transcends space.

The evidence indicates (and the industry studies corroborate) that the commercial introduction of the three-quarter-inch videocassette in 1971 (with its inherent accessibility characteristics) led to a diversity of corporate senders and receivers. The accessibility/standardization equation is echoed by Eric Havelock (1976) in *Origins of Western Literacy*. Havelock contended that because of the visual standardization of oral communication via the development of the Greek alphabet, Western man was given greater freedom of novelty: science, industrialization, and the general democratization of knowledge. The effect of the new communications technology was to allow increasingly larger numbers of people (i.e., the process of adoption) to communicate in writing through the act of reading. Similarly, the development of the three-quarter-inch videocassette, with its attendant lightness, portability, ease, and multiplicity of use for production, editing, and distribution allowed larger numbers of people (i.e., the process of adoption) to communicate electronically through the act of viewing. The process of videotape's adoption in the nonbroadcast market context continues to this day.

6

The Home Video Market

The practical development of the videotape recorder was a natural outgrowth of the rapidly growing audiotape recorder industry in the United States. Stimulated by the demands of the professional broadcast, educational, and nonbroadcast industries, audiotape recorder manufacturers naturally began to explore the possibilities of adapting existing technologies and knowledge toward the objective of producing a videotape recorder and playback capability.

Ampex, which had been the first company to produce a professionally acceptable audiotape recorder and playback in the United States, used the momentum and expertise it had accrued in the audio medium to build a new technological and marketing beachhead in the new visual medium. As the developer of the first practical professional videotape recorder in the mid-1950s, the California-based company was able to consolidate its power as the dominant entity in the broadcast and other organizational markets. Ampex clearly reigned supreme in the professional arena. However, other companies in the United States and overseas began to explore the marketing potential of this new video technology for home use.

The Sony Corporation, already in the process of establishing itself as a major force in the manufacturing and marketing of other consumer electronics products, began research in the home video field in 1953. Sony's management believed "there should be no reason why people would not want to have a video recorder at home just as they had audiotape recorders for home, personal use" (Morita, 1986, p. 111).

By 1958, MITI (the Japanese Ministry of International Trade and Industry) had created a roundtable (composed of Sony and other major Japanese consumer electronics manufacturers) to coordinate research on videotape recorders. This comprehensive industry approach to product development was characteristic of the way in which the Japanese government encouraged its private sector to further its economic objectives (the restrictive nature of U.S. antitrust laws made it virtually impossible for American consumer electronics companies to cooperate in a similar way). Partially due to these joint efforts—as well as through their own individual research activities—Sony, Matsushita Electric Corporation, Toshiba, and JVC were able to develop prototype videotape recorders by 1959. These units utilized a helical scanning system that allowed a greater amount of information to be recorded on the tape than had been previously possible using Ampex's transverse scanning system while reducing the physical wear on the tape heads. The helical scanning system is the one used in most of today's videocassette recorders (Lardner, 1987, p. 62).

While Japan was conducting this research, Ampex was making major inroads into Japanese educational and professional broadcasting markets with its patented recording and playback system. To neutralize Ampex's success in their country, Japanese manufacturers began producing and marketing copies of Ampex videotape recorders. In 1964, unable to convince the Japanese government to stop these patent violations, Ampex signed an exclusive agreement with Toshiba, forming a joint venture called Toshiba Ampex K.K., to manufacture and market the U.S.-designed videotape recorder in Japan ("Ampex and Toshiba," 1964). The problem of patent infringement by other Japanese companies ended abruptly.

Four years earlier (1960), Ampex had signed an agreement with Sony to give the U.S. firm access to the American-invented transistor technology that had reached state-of-the-art development in Japan. In return for Sony's designing and supplying transistorized circuits for a portable version of Ampex's bulky machine, the U.S. company had awarded Sony the rights to use the Ampex patents for the manufacture of videotape recorders for nonbroadcast markets (Scherick, 1987, p. 63). Sony had quickly exploited this agreement and introduced its own videotape recorder in 1961. Soon after, it had begun to market its first helical scanning videotape recorder (PV-100), which was bought by American Airlines in 1964 to show first-run feature films on videotape during cross-country flights ("Airline TV," 1964).

Belatedly, Ampex awakened to the sales potential of consumer markets. It introduced its first consumer videotape recorder through the Neiman-Marcus (department store) Christmas catalog in 1963. The price was a daunting $30,000 per unit (Lardner, 1987, p. 65). Within a year, many more entrants announced their intent to introduce videotape recorders for the consumer market. The first videotape recorder to reach that market in the United States was developed by a British company, Wesgrove Electrics Ltd. This machine for the home, priced at $1,100 ("Tape-It-Yourself TV," 1965), allowed twenty-five minutes to be recorded on each side of an eleven and-a-half-inch open reel. The company also offered a budget-priced build-it-yourself version for $450 ("British-made Wesgrove," 1965).

Another videotape recorder was developed by the ITT Research Center of the Illinois Institute of Technology; a third was introduced by Fairchild Camera and Instrument. Both of these systems utilized one-quarter-inch audiotape on open reels ("Home Video Recording at Slow Speed," 1964). Prospects for the Fairchild system seemed especially exciting to U.S. television-set manufacturers, causing a leading industry publication to note, "It seems certain that a major new consumer electronics product is now on its way" ("Fairchild," 1964).

A previously announced British entrant, Telcan, continued to plan its product's U.S. introduction, utilizing the feature film marketing resources of the Cinerama organization ("Outlook for Telcan," 1964). And in June 1964 Par Ltd. demonstrated its Par-Vision system, claiming its home videotape recorder could be produced to sell for $300-$400 and its playback-only model could sell for less than $200 ("Home Video Recording at Thirty IPS," 1964). Neither model made it successfully to the U.S. market.

In the fall of 1964 two new European companies announced they were also introducing home videotape recorders. They were an Austrian subsidiary of Philips (the Dutch consumer electronics firm) and a German company, Loewe-Opta, both of which planned to reach the U.S. consumer market, even though their suggested retail prices were $2,500-$3,000 ("Two Made in Europe," 1964).

In 1963, two years after Ampex introduced its first $30,000 consumer model in the United States, Sony offered Americans what it described as "the first home videorecorder," a one-half-inch open-reel videotape format that recorded in black-and-white only. The portable model cost $995. The console version, which contained a built-in clock to record programs automatically, was $1,250 ("Sony Launches," 1965). That same year, Ampex announced the introduction of a home videotape recorder using a one-inch tape format. Its retail price was $1,095 ("Video Recorder", 1965).

Ampex and Sony were now battling each other in U.S. consumer, business, and educational markets. Subsequently, Ampex repudiated its original agreement with Sony and sued the Japanese company for copyright infringement in 1966. Sony countersued, charging restraint of trade. The suits were settled out of court two years later (Lardner, 1987, p. 68).

While Ampex and Sony fought, the market for home video became crowded with aspiring suppliers. Increasing numbers of U.S., European, and Japanese manufacturers—including Precision Apparatus, Defense Electronics, Wollensak, and the 3M Company—announced plans to produce and market videotape recorders designed to exploit the potentially lucrative American market. Most, however, never survived beyond the prototype stage. Other companies—including General Electric, Delmonico International, and Concord Electronics Corporation—announced their intentions to enter the U.S. home video market with products made for their labels by such Japanese giants as Sony, JVC, and Matsushita Electric ("Two More VTRs," 1966). Their decisions to import videotape recorder technology rather than to develop it at home contributed substantially to the trend that ultimately caused American companies to abdicate their roles as innovators and leaders in the design of consumer electronics products.

UNITED STATES ATTEMPTS TO MAINTAIN CONTROL OF HOME VIDEO

CBS, using the research and development resources of CBS Laboratories (under the leadership of Dr. Peter Goldmark), continued to look for a way to maintain control of the home video market. The CBS system, called "Electronic Video Recording" (EVR), utilized a form of photographic film in a cassette. Because it was radically different from the other competing formats incorporating magnetic tape, the EVR was introduced in December 1968 with major fanfare ("CBS's EVR Launching," 1968). Twentieth Century Fox Film Corporation negotiated a deal to distribute Fox films on EVR cartridges for rental purposes five years after their theatrical release. Darryl F. Zanuck, then chairman of Fox, described the EVR as being as important an entertainment technology as "the talkies, color movies and Cinemascope" ("Color EVR in Fall," 1970). However, the EVR never achieved any significant success and was ultimately abandoned by CBS in December 1971 ("CBS Out," 1971).

RCA, having been beaten by Ampex in the race to produce the first successful videotape recorder for the broadcast industry, then turned its energies to the home video market. The result of its labors, "SelectaVision," was demonstrated for the press in October 1969. RCA officials assured the journalists SelectaVision would be introduced to the U.S. consumer market in 1972, but the video technology never left RCA's laboratory. RCA ultimately embraced a Japanese system and successfully marketed it under the RCA label ("RCA's SelectaVision," 1969).

The final attempt to gain U.S. dominance in home video was initiated in June 1969, when Playtape and Avco Industries joined to form a company called Cartridge TV, Inc. and announced plans to market a videotape recorder and player system, "Cartrivision," that used one-quarter-inch magnetic tape contained in a cartridge ("Playtape and Avco," 1969). A number of major U.S. television–set manufacturers began to make these units. Sears Roebuck and Montgomery Ward both committed their massive distribution and sales resources to support the system throughout the country ("Sears, Ward Embrace Cartrivision," 1971).

After suffering a number of production and marketing problems, Cartridge TV, Inc. exhausted its financial resources and halted its operations in July 1973 ("Cartridge TV," 1973). DeLuca (1980, p. 251) suggested that a primary reason why Cartrivision went bankrupt so quickly was that it cut its profit margin below acceptable business limits in order to keep its retail prices within a range that the company's market researchers believed was affordable by the public. He also stated that in 1972, when Cartrivision was introduced, "no one much cared about being able to record television programs for themselves" (p. 252). This consumer behavior pattern clearly changed three years later when the Betamax was successfully introduced, primarily as a means to record and time-shift television programing.

After the failure of Cartrivision, no other serious attempt was made to control the development and manufacture of home video by U.S. manufacturers. By the time Sony launched the Betamax into the U.S. consumer market in the fall of 1975, American manufacturers of home entertainment products (like Zenith and RCA) were no longer investing in videocassette recorder research and development. They had abandoned their leadership positions in this field and assumed the primary role of distributors and marketing organizations for Japanese products ("Japan Moves," 1977).

During the late 1960s and early 1970s, there seemed to be a consensus in the consumer electronics industry that home video was a technology with enormous market potential. By 1970, announcements had been made about twenty different systems, almost none of which was compatible with any other. This lack of standardization was universally decried, yet each electronics company believed its concept should set the industry standard ("Videoplayers," 1970).

Responding to this problem in 1971, the EIAJ formed a committee of engineers who were charged with the task of developing a standardized format for the one-half-inch videotape recorder. With the adoption of an EIAJ standard in 1972 a new flood of one-half-inch videotape recorders entered the market. Sony, Panasonic, JVC, and Hitachi all produced machines. However, the short playing time (thirty minutes), bulkiness, and high cost ($1,000) of the machines limited their appeal and none of them gained popular acceptance. This represented the last successful attempt by the Japanese government to establish a universal homevideo standard (DeLuca, 1980, pp. 82–85).

SONY AND THE U-MATIC

Among Japanese manufacturers, Sony had taken an early lead in developing a practical videotape cassette recorder. It had concentrated on reducing both the size of its videocassette recorder and the width of its videotape. This research led Sony to develop a new three-quarter-inch videotape system called the "U-matic," which was demonstrated in 1969.

Sony was not the only Japanese manufacturer working on a marketable three-quarter-inch videocassette recorder. Matsushita and JVC were also well advanced in product development. However, in 1970, at a meeting during a trade show in Osaka, the three companies formally agreed to collaborate on their research, using Sony's U-matic as the primary design concept. They also agreed to share without restrictions all future technical innovations that were developed relating to videocassette recorders. This unrestricted pooling of technical research theoretically remained in effect in the following years as the three competitors pursued improvements in one-half-inch videocassette recorder technology. In practice, however, the companies generally went their own ways after 1970 (Nayak and Ketteringham, 1986, pp. 26–27).

The Sony U-matic was successful because of its quality picture image and the simplicity of its system, which used a one-hour tape cassette about the size of a hardcover book. The U-matic was quickly embraced by the broadcasting world for most applications to replace the two-inch-wide tape units that Ampex had introduced in the late 1950s. It was also adopted by the business and educational sectors as their primary visual vehicle, which virtually made obsolete the 16mm film format that had been previously used (Morita, 1986, pp. 111–12).

During the U-matic's 1969 press introduction in New York, Sony's Akio Morita labeled the machine the "color video phonograph" of the 1970s. In addition to positioning the unit in the professional field, Morita seemed to be trying to preempt the competitive incursions of the CBS, RCA, and Cartrivision home video systems when he said that the U-matic would retail for less than $500 after its introduction.

Its actual introductory price was more than $2,500. He also proposed both a video cartridge trade-in scheme, that would allow owners to exchange blank for prerecorded tapes for a fee at selected retail stores, and a special tape cassette to be used by video rental stores, that would incorporate a counter to record how many times a tape had been played ("Sony Enters," 1969). But these ideas were never implemented.

Sony began to market the U-matic in the United States in 1971. Matsushita and JVC followed soon after with their versions of the U-matic. But Sony quickly gained a major share of the broadcasting, business, and educational markets. Although Matsushita and JVC exerted strenuous efforts to sell their U-matic versions, they never overtook Sony and remained minor entries in the three-quarter-inch videocassette recorder category. Despite aggressive marketing efforts by all three manufacturers, as well as by the firms that subsequently licensed the design, a significant consumer demand for the product never materialized. The U-matic was considered too big and expensive for home use. Even when the U-matic's retail price was subsequently reduced to $1,395, the unit was still too expensive for all but a small affluent group. The price never dropped to the $500 level. Sony made a modest profit in the consumer market on its three-quarter-inch videocassette recorder, but all of the other manufacturers of the machine lost money (Nayak & Ketteringham, 1986, p. 28).

THE VIDEO DISC

As Japanese videocassette recorder manufacturers and their U.S. licensees searched for the profits they expected to find in the U.S. home video market, another video technology surfaced. The video disc was introduced and it threatened to challenge the videocassette recorder as a primary home video medium. Philips, the Dutch consumer electronics manufacturer, first demonstrated its disc in 1972. It utilized a laser beam to lift data from a disc about the size and shape of a longplaying phonograph record. The disc not only offered superior picture quality but also allowed users to store and scan 45,000 individual images on each side ("Philips VLP," 1972). However, Philips' disc and all of the other discs that were developed later were playback-only machines. The video disc lacked a recording capability.

Three months later, MCA, the Los Angeles-based entertainment conglomerate, announced it was introducing its own video disc format, "DiscoVision". Its capability closely resembled Philips' disc ("DiscoVision," 1972). Philips and MCA subsequently agreed to merge their technologies. However, by that time they were confronting RCA, which had decided to introduce its own version of the video disc in an attempt to dominate the U.S. home video marketplace ("Video disc Battle-lines," 1975). RCA's disc system, "SelectaVision," used a stylus in the track of a disc similar in size to the Philips/MCA version (Head & Sterling, 1982, p. 82).

The marketing battle between these giants continued into the early 1980s but waned when it became obvious consumers were not interested in any home video device that could not record as well as play back. By the end of 1981, DiscoVision, with estimated losses of $30 million, was dismantling its organization (Lardner, 1987, p. 206). RCA finally abandoned its video disc system in 1984 (Donnelly, 1986, p. 116). It was estimated RCA lost $183 million on the venture ("Disk System Loses," 1982, p. 4).

Late in 1989, several major European and Japanese consumer electronics companies introduced a new generation of laser video disc players selling for $500 or less. These new models integrated both the video disc capability as well as the ability to play audio compact discs (CDs). It is yet to be proven that the American consumer is ready to embrace a play-only video technology, even with its added audio capacity (A New Spin, 1989).

As the marketers at Sony, Matsushita, and JVC were attempting to persuade the consumer market to accept the three-quarter-inch videocassette recorder as the home video standard, their research and development departments—as well as those of other electronics companies in Japan, the United States, and Europe—were struggling to simplify and miniaturize the videotape cassette recorder. A few companies produced prototypes utilizing a one-quarter-inch videotape format. However, most began to focus on the one-half-inch videotape cassette as the most likely to succeed.

JVC AND THE VHS FORMAT

In 1971, abandoning the three-quarter-inch U-matic format as a template for future home videocassette recorder designs, JVC began the development program that led to the creation of the now dominant VHS format (Nayak & Ketteringham, 1986, p. 28). Shortly after launching the U-matic in the United States, Sony also began research that evolved from the concept of the three-quarter-inch format videocassette recorder into the one-half-inch Betamax format videocassette recorder that started the home video revolution (Lardner, 1987, pp. 91–93).

JVC, the acronym for Victor Company of Japan, Ltd., had been formed after World War II by the U.S.-owned Victor Talking Machines Company, a unit of RCA. It was acquired in 1953 by the Matsushita Electric Industrial Company, Ltd. and was established as an independent subsidiary.

Originally JVC was primarily involved in the manufacture of records and high-fidelity phonographs. The company built its first videotape recorder in 1961, five years after Ampex had launched its phenomenally successful videotape recorder in 1956. JVC continued to manufacture videotape recorders in the following years, but it never achieved the marketplace success scored by Matsushita (its corporate parent) or Sony. Compared with the financial and human resources Sony committed to the development of a practical home videocassette recorder, JVC's efforts were feeble (Nayak & Ketteringham, 1986, pp. 23–28).

A small group of JVC engineers, led by Yuma Shiraishi and Shizuo Yakano, began to explore new approaches to the project. The engineers established a list of twelve goals to serve as a continuing guide for their exploration. These goals for the videocassette recorder were the following:

For the videocassette recorder itself

1. It should be connectable to an ordinary television.
2. It should be able to reproduce in quality the same image and sound as an ordinary television receiver.
3. It should have a minimum recording time of two hours.
4. It should be compatible with other manufacturers' videocasette recorders so that the tape is interchangeable.
5. It should have a wide range of functions, such as use with prerecorded software and/or a video camera.

For use in private homes

6. It should not be too expensive.
7. It should be easy to operate.
8. The operating costs (tape, etc.) should be low.

For the manufacturer

9. It should be reasonably easy to produce.
10. It should be designed so that parts can be used in a number of models.
11. It should be easy to service.

For society

12. It should serve as the transmitter of information and culture (pp. 28–31).

The JVC team produced its first working prototype by 1974. It was at that point that Sony's management approached JVC's parent company, Matsushita, to discuss the possibility of agreement on a single format, the Betamax.

THE BETAMAX IS BORN

While the final form of the three-quarter-inch U-matic videocassette recorder was the result of the combined thinking of Sony, JVC, and Matsushita, the development of the Betamax was exclusively a Sony project. Sony had maintained a tradition of independence since its birth in 1946. Under the leadership of its founder, Masaru Ibuka, it had challenged traditional Japanese electronics companies in Japanese, as well as worldwide, markets and had quickly grown to become a leading force in consumer electronics. It never became the largest manufacturer in the business, but it did build a formidable reputation as a technological innovator with a shrewd sense of the market. This was reflected most dramatically in its development and introduction of the Betamax (Lardner, 1987, p. 52).

The Betamax was created in Sony's laboratories under the leadership of Nobutoshi Kihara, the engineer responsible for the development of the U-matic. Ibuka had set the standard when he asked Kihara and his associates to create a consumer videocassette recorder that would utilize a cassette no larger than a paperback book. By mid-1974, a prototype was built and the Betamax was born. Beta is a Japanese word describing a thickly applied brush stroke that totally covers the surface being painted (pp. 91–92).

At this time, Sony proposed that RCA consider the Betamax as its candidate for the one-half-inch videocassette recorder category. This proposal came as RCA was struggling to bring its own patented one-half-inch system, MagTape, to market but was beginning to doubt its potential for success. Nevertheless, RCA was reluctant to strike a deal with Sony to distribute the Betamax because the U.S. company's marketing research indicated Americans would not embrace a videocassette recorder that could record for only one hour. At this point, Sony's chairman, Morita, was adamant that a one-hour capacity was sufficient. RCA finally abandoned its MagTape system, but it did not accept Sony's Betamax, preferring to wait until a system more attuned to U.S. home video market needs was available ("Sony HVR," 1975).

In the fall of 1974 Sony proposed to Matsushita and JVC that they jointly develop a one-half-inch videocassette recorder, as they had previously collaborated on the U-matic. This time, however, Sony presented a production, rather than a prototype, unit, for the Betamax was already being manufactured at Sony facilities in preparation for mass marketing. The managements of Matsushita and JVC knew Sony had discussed a working relationship with RCA and had been rejected before approaching them. They also recognized they were being offered no alternative. They could either accept Sony's finished product or reject the offer. After a series of acrimonious meetings, they finally advised Sony in May 1976 that they were going their own way, strongly implying that they would be using the JVC VHS home video format. By this time, Sony had already launched the Betamax (Nayak & Ketteringham, 1986, pp. 38–40).

In May 1975, nine months after initiating discussions with its competitors about a common one-half-inch videocassette recorder format, Sony introduced the first Betamax videocassette recorder to the Japanese consumer market. It was an immediate success. The American introduction took place in November 1975 (Lyons, 1976, p. 209).

BETAMAX VERSUS VHS

In the spring of 1976 Sony made one last attempt to persuade the VHS advocates to accept the Beta format. It urged the Japanese government, through MITI, to intercede in the dispute in the interest of achieving a single standard. But meetings of industry representatives, held at MITI's request in an attempt to resolve the issue amicably, were unsuccessful. Neither side would abandon its home video concept. The battle lines between the Beta and VHS forces were drawn (Lardner, 1987, p. 157).

Even before negotiations between Sony and the VHS forces were formally ended, the two sides had begun seeking allies in the approaching confrontation. Hitachi, Mitsubishi, and Sharp were the first to align themselves publicly with JVC and its VHS format. They began marketing their branded products in December 1976. JVC had launched its own version of the two-hour VHS videocassette recorder in Japan in early October 1976. Its introductory price was the U.S. equivalent of $885, almost $200 less than Sony's one-hour Betamax videocassette recorder deck ("JVC to Market," 1976). JVC's parent, Matsushita, followed with an announcement of its commitment to VHS one month after JVC launched its VHS videocassette recorder (Nayak & Ketteringham, 1986, p. 42).

While Sony began limited distribution of the Betamax in the United States in late 1975, the company did not start aggressively marketing the unit to the American consumer until early 1976. Marcella Rosen (personal communication, January 25, 1988), senior vice president and managing director of media services at N. W. Ayer, recalled that the broadcast industry largely ignored Sony's new consumer product because it seemed to be essentially a product appealing primarily to the affluent. Sony's first advertisement in New York promoted the $1,300 Betamax as a "video time-shift machine" for recording and playing back broadcast television programs. Beta one-hour blank tape cassettes sold for $15.95 ("First Home VTR Deck," 1976). Three months later, Sony's chairman, Morita, attempted to minimize criticism of the Betamax's single hour of recording time. He announced Sony had built a prototype automatic cassette changer capable of providing ten hours of continuous recording ("Sanyo Home VTR," 1976). This product never received significant distribution and was withdrawn from the market when Sony increased the Betamax's recording time from one hour to two hours.

As the conflict became heated, *Television Digest* reported a "Stop Betamax Move" was forming in Japan. The movement, it said, was triggered by Japanese manufacturer's concerns about the impact of the Betamax on the consumer market. The JVC VHS recorder could be nominated as the Japanese electronics industry's "Stop Sony" machine, the article concluded ("Stop-Beta Move," 1976). Sony's chairman, Morita, responded to this challenge, saying that "another company cannot win" against Sony's magnetic tape experience and know-how. Sony spokesmen expressed confidence the Betamax would gain the same worldwide acceptance as the three-quarter-inch U-matic. "These incompatible machines are just an ego-trip—they're slitting their own throats," said Sonam's (Sony's U.S. division) president, Harvey Schein ("Behind Sony," 1976).

Sony's cause was significantly strengthened in February 1977 when Zenith Radio Corporation, the largest U.S. television-set manufacturer, announced it had entered into a licensing agreement to market but not manufacture the Betamax to American consumers and to support the effort with a major advertising campaign ("Zenith Sets, Fall Rollout," 1977). Later that day it was revealed that Toshiba and Sanyo, two other major Japanese manufacturers, had joined the Beta family (Nayak & Ketteringham, 1986, p. 43).

The VHS forces won the next round a month later. RCA, the second largest U.S. manufacturer of television sets, announced it had signed a contract to market Matsushita-built VHS format videocassette recorders in the United States. RCA also announced it would be the first company in the United States to offer consumers four-hour recording capability with its models of VHS format videocassette recorders. Sony's Morita quickly responded with a statesmanlike comment, welcoming "all manufacturers into the new market." He added, "With their millions of dollars for advertising and promotion [they] will develop a greater consumer awareness of this new entertainment format" ("Japan Moves," 1977, p. 9). Two months later,

Magnavox and Sylvania, two other major U.S. television-set producers, also committed themselves to marketing Matsushita's four-hour version of the VHS format videocassette recorder ("Magnavox, Sylvania," 1977). Sears Roebuck joined the VHS group a month later.

Jack Wayman, a retired senior vice president of the Electronic Industries Association and key figure in the development of the videocassette recorder, recalled that "1977 was when the VCR really kicked off and became a commercial consumer product" (J. Wayman, personal communication, February 3, 1988). By June 1977 (one and one-half years after Sony formally entered the U.S. market), Japanese-made videocassette recorders were being sold under fifteen different U.S. manufacturers' and marketers' brand names.

The country that invented the videotape recorder was now importing all of its consumer videocassette recorder equipment from Japan. The Japanese, who had previously achieved their consumer electronics success by capitalizing on the results of American industry's research and development, were now America's primary consumer electronics suppliers. Increasingly, American consumer electronics manufacturers were acting as marketers for imported products, rather than as pioneers in new product development ("Home VTRs," 1977).

THE BETAMAX CASE

Fifteen months after Sony introduced the first Betamax to America in September 1975, a lawsuit charging Sony with copyright infringement was filed in Los Angeles Federal District Court by MCA/Universal Studios and Walt Disney Productions. In addition to Sony, its American subsidiary, Sonam; its U.S. advertising agency, Doyle Dane Bernbach; four Southern California Betamax retailers; and a Betamax owner named William Griffiths were also named as defendants.

The two film studios were challenging Sony's legal right to encourage and provide a way for Americans to videotape copyrighted material at home on their Betamax videocassette recorders. More specifically, they were challenging Sony's right to provide the American public with the physical means to copy shows, such as *Kojak* and *Columbo*, that these studios owned and that were then appearing on the U.S. television networks ("Copyright Suit Challenge," 1976). In fact, the studios' suit called for anyone who had recorded their motion pictures (on a Betamax) to be forced to surrender those tapes for destruction ("Lawsuit Attacks Sales," 1976). There was no question that Sony was actively promoting the Betamax as a device for recording television shows off the air. DeLuca (1980, p. 254) noted Sony's strategy was to persuade viewers equipped with a Betamax

Figure 6.1
Early Advertising for Sony Betamax

MAKE YOUR OWN TV SCHEDULE.

Sony's Betamax can automatically videotape your favorite show for you to play back anytime you want.

Now you can watch anything you want to watch anytime you want to watch it.

Because Sony's revolutionary Betamax deck—which hooks up to any television set—can automatically videotape your favorite show (even when you're not home) for you to play back anytime you want.

(By the way, you can reuse our one-hour tape cassettes simply by recording over them.)

But possibly the most amazing thing of all is this: Now you can actually see two programs that are on at the same time. Because Betamax can videotape something off one channel while you're watching another channel. So, after you're finished watching one show, you can play back a tape of the other show.

Imagine. Watching the Late Show in the morning. Or a soap opera in the evening. Or whatever whenever. What power!

BETAMAX®
"IT'S A SONY."

See a demonstration of Betamax at:

Source: Sony Corporation of America, Parkridge, NJ. Reprinted with permission of Sony Corporation of America.

Figure 6.2
Early Advertising for Sony Betamax

NOW YOUR KIDS DON'T HAVE TO MISS MONDAY NIGHT FOOTBALL BECAUSE THEY'RE STUDYING FOR A TUESDAY MORNING EXAM.

 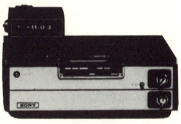

They never again have to be torn between studying and watching their favorite TV show.

Not if you own Sony's revolutionary Betamax Deck.

Because Betamax, which hooks up to any TV set, can automatically videotape a show while you're doing something else—so you can play it back later, at your leisure.

And if you think that's extraordinary, just listen to this.

Say there are two programs you want to watch on at the same time (as so often happens).

Well, believe it or not, with Sony's Betamax you can see both of them. Because Betamax can actually videotape something off one channel while you're watching another channel. Then, when you're finished watching one show, all you do is push some buttons and play back a tape of the show you would have otherwise missed.

Our one-hour tapes are reusable—just record over them, and use them over and over again. (Or, if you wish, don't record over them and build a library of your favorite shows.)

Now if only you could get the kids to eat right.

BETAMAX®
"IT'S A SONY."

See a demonstration of Betamax at:

Source: Sony Corporation of America, Parkridge, NJ. Reprinted with permission of Sony Corporation of America.

Figure 6.3
Early Advertising for Sony Betamax

YOU SHOULD CONTROL TV, IT SHOULDN'T CONTROL YOU.

"Can we eat a little early, dear? There's something on at seven o'clock I want to watch."

"A PTA meeting tonight? I'm going to miss that show I've been wanting to see."

"Can I do my homework later, mommy? My favorite show is going on."

What in the world are we doing to ourselves? Our lives are being governed, to too great an extent, by TV schedules.

Sony's Betamax: It videotapes a TV show so you can play it back anytime you want.

Well, they needn't be any longer. Thanks to Sony's Betamax videotape deck.

The SL-8200 Betamax, which plugs into any TV set, can videotape any show you like, up to two hours, while you're doing something else. Even when you're out of the house, by setting the optional automatic timer.

So you can play it back at your convenience. And as if that weren't enough, Betamax can also videotape something off one channel while you're watching another channel—for those

Your kids can see the shows they want at the times you want.

times when there are two things on simultaneously that you want to watch.

Our tapes, of course, are reusable. You just rerecord over them, and use them over and over again.

With Sony's Betamax, you'll experience a sense of power you've never felt before.

On nights you're out, Betamax's timer can be set to automatically videotape your favorite show.

SONY BETAMAX®
THE LEADER IN VIDEO RECORDING

Source: Sony Corporation of America, Parkridge, NJ. Reprinted with permission of Sony Corporation of America.

Figure 6.4
Early Advertising for Sony Betamax

THIS AMAZING MACHINE CAN ADD HOURS TO YOUR DAY.

The hours you spend watching television are often the hours you could be using to get other things done.

What to do? Simple. Add those hours to your day with a Sony Betamax home videorecorder.

Our new SL-8600 Betamax gives you up to three hours recording time on one L-750 videocassette —which is as long as you're likely to need.

It plugs into your TV and lets you videotape shows while you're doing something else. Even while you're out of the house, by using our built-in 24-hour LED digital automatic timer. And you can play them back at your convenience.

And if there are two shows on at the same time that you want to see, Betamax can handle that one too. Because it can actually videotape something off one channel while you're watching another channel. And if you're taping the show you're watching, you'll be glad to know it's got a remote control pause button. Pretty amazing!

And here's what else you're going to get from Betamax the Sony name and

all it stands for 20 years of experience and dependability. In fact, we've not only sold more *home* videorecorders, we've also sold more to broadcasters and industry than any other consumer manufacturer. Plus we make all our own videorecorders *and* our own parts. (And we're the only consumer manufacturer who makes our own tapes. In fact, we have just built a multimillion-dollar tape plant in Dothan, Alabama.) You probably didn't think you could be in two places at once. Well, now you know you can. You see, stretching the hours in a day really is easy. If you own a Betamax.

SONY® BETAMAX®
THE LEADER IN VIDEO RECORDING

Come in and see a demonstration at your authorized Sony Betamax dealer:

Source: Sony Corporation of America, Parkridge, NJ. Reprinted with permission of Sony Corporation of America.

to watch their favorite shows at their convenience instead of when the show was actually on the air. Sony also encouraged viewers to watch one show while recording another. (Figures 6.1-6.4 show early advertising for Sony Betamax.)

The Betamax case (as it came to be called) worked its way through the U.S. Federal Court system for eight years until it was finally decided by the U.S. Supreme Court in January 1984. During that period, sales of videocassette recorders to U.S. dealers climbed from 55,000 units in 1976 to more than seven and one-half million units in 1984 ("Color TV Analogy," 1984). The Betamax case pitted Sony—and ultimately the entire consumer electronics industry—against some of the most powerful forces in the entertainment business. It became a struggle between representatives of entrenched media technologies (motion pictures and the broadcast television networks) and advocates of a new media technology (the videocassette recorder) that was clearly perceived as a significant threat to the power and future prosperity of the older ones. And by the time the battle was over, the consumer videocassette recorder had evolved from being an expensive electronic toy for a small group of faddists to playing a major role in the life-styles of millions of Americans.

The case was initiated because MCA/Universal's president, Sidney Sheinberg, had become convinced Sony was marketing a machine whose prime reason for existence was to duplicate copyrighted material. In fact, the headline of the original newspaper advertisement that was submitted for approval to MCA/Universal in September 1976 by Sony's advertising agency, Doyle Dane Bernbach, emphasized that Betamax owners could videotape one of Universal's television shows, *Kojak*, while watching another, *Columbo* (Lardner, 1987, p. 21).

MCA's Sheinberg saw a technology designed to violate his company's copyrights. On the other hand, Sony's Morita saw a technology designed to free people from the constraints of time. Morita's concept of "time-shift" had been the central reason for the development of the Betamax. "We established our marketing policy to promote the new concept of time-shift," said Morita in his biography, *Made in Japan.* "It was my idea that we had to create a market for the videocassette recorder by educating people and giving them new ideas. . . . With the VCR, television is like a magazine—you can control your own schedule" (Morita, 1986, p. 208).

In October 1979, three years after the Betamax case began, Federal District Judge Warren J. Ferguson ruled in California court that "noncommercial use of home video recorders to record television broadcasts is lawful." Sony had won the first legal round. Commenting on the case, a Sony spokesman suggested that a major influence on MCA/Universal's original decision to sue Sony might have been MCA's planned introduction of its video disc playback system (Lindsey, 1979b). At that time, the video disc was regarded as a possible rival for the consumer's home entertainment dollar.

In October 1981 a U.S. Appeals Court reversed Judge Ferguson's ruling. An article in the *New York Times* reported the court found that "videotape recording of copyrighted television programs, even if it is done at home only for private use, is an infringement of rights of those who own programs" (Feder, 1981, p. 1). The article suggested that millions of American consumers who used videotape machines to record programs from their television sets could be sued for damages, as could the companies that manufactured videocassette recorders, the stores that sold them, and the advertising agencies that. encouraged consumers to buy them ("Private Videotaping," 1981).

MCA's initial response came two weeks later. The company filed another copyright infringement suit in Los Angeles Federal District Court. This suit's targets included virtually the entire U.S. and Japanese videocassette recorder industries; forty-two defendants were cited. MCA's suit specifically charged the defendants with "inducing buyers to omit television commercials . . . (and) skip over recorded commercials by use of the fast-forward and other controls" ("Battle Lines Form," 1981, p. 9).

On a less overt level, both sides began to organize campaigns aimed at influencing favorable legislation in the U.S. Congress affecting the videocassette recorder and videotapes. Sony enlisted the support of the Electronic Industries Association (EIA) and sixteen other videocassette recorder marketers, who instituted a Washington-based "Right to Tape" lobbying coalition (p. 9). MCA and all the other major Hollywood film studios banded together and designated their industry trade group, the Motion Picture Association of America (MPAA), as their advocate on Capitol Hill. At this point, the goal of the film companies had shifted from trying to stop the use of the videocassette recorder to gaining a royalty on video-cassette recorders and blank tapes, as well as to controlling the burgeoning videotape rental business in the United States through modified copyright legislation (Lardner, 1987, pp. 206-7).

The goals of the videocassette recorder coalition were to win a reversal of the appeals court decision and to encourage legislation supporting Americans' right to videotape. These goals were not without supporters in Congress. One day after the appeals court ruled against Sony, bills were introduced in the House of Representatives and the Senate calling for the federal courts to "stop intruding into the homes of millions of Americans." Congressional hearings were initiated to consider the videocassette recorder issue.

As the MPAA asked movie and television stars to testify on the industry's behalf, Sony ran advertisements in twenty-three major U.S. newspapers with the headline, "What Time Is It?" The copy discussed man's historic "battle against the dictates and restraints of time," suggesting that the home videocassette recorder had succeeded in mastering time. It then warned, "Now your freedom to use this tool is being threatened by a court decision" ("Senate Hearings," 1981, p. 7).

None of the House and Senate bills, which were amended several times, ever reached the floor of Congress for a vote. However, they fanned the flames of public awareness of the technology at a time when the videocassette recorders' U.S. sales were accelerating. It is possible the controversy initiated by MCA/Universal actually enlarged the market and caused even more consumers to buy videocassette recorders than might have otherwise.

The final stage of the Betamax legal conflict began in June 1982 when the U.S. Supreme Court announced it had decided to review the ruling of the lower court. The battle ended in January 1984 when the Supreme Court reversed the appeals court's ruling against Sony, voting five to four that "neither the consumers who tape television programs for their own use nor companies that make and sell video recorders violate federal copyright law" (Greenhouse, 1984, p. 1). This decision essentially denied the major U.S. motion picture companies any compensation from the sale of blank tapes and videocassette recorders in the United States (Scherick, 1987, p. 64).

THE PRERECORDED VIDEOTAPE MARKET

Gould (1956) acknowledged the potential of the videocassette recorder and playback machine as a new delivery system for feature films only one week after it was publicly unveiled in the United States: "Why not pick up the new full-length motion picture at the corner drugstore and then run it through one's home TV receiver?" (p. 13).

The Hollywood executives and other producers of programing began indicating an awareness of the videocassette recorder's possibilities as a new distribution outlet for their material long before the product had become viable for the mass market. The major motion picture studios had begun exploring concepts for the use of home videotapes as a possible medium for movie distribution as early as 1964. Paramount Senior Vice President Paul Raibourn had told an industry symposium then that when the home videotape player eventually arrives in quantity, "the motion picture producer is going to have another way of exhibiting his pictures to the public for direct payment" ("Video Tape Movies," 1964, p. 7). The first publicly announced effort to capitalize on the prerecorded home video market was made at a U.S. record industry trade show in 1966 when an executive of Audio Fidelity Records told the press his company was issuing one-hour videotapes that could be played back on an early version of a Sony reel-to-reel videotape recorder. A mail-order "Video Tape Club" was planned, with musical videotapes to be sold for $49.95. There were no more than 2,000 videotape recorders in home use in the United States at the time ("Birth of a New Era," 1956).

Ampex, the pioneer videotape developer, and Advanced Management Research, Inc., were the first companies to explore the educational market. In 1968 they offered two videotaped courses, "Marketing the Computer" and "Fundamentals of Finance and Accounting for Nonfinancial Executives." Each was four to five hours long, broken into thirty-minute segments, and was offered on one-inch videotape for $3,175. Each could also be rented for fifteen days for half the purchase price ("Courses by Videotape," 1968).

The first serious attempt to exploit the still-untapped prerecorded videocassette recorder market occurred in 1970 when Avco announced that, as part of its marketing program for Cartrivision, it would also sell a full line of feature films on nonrewindable, prerecorded videotapes designed so that a viewer could watch a cassette only once before returning it to the dealer for a credit toward a subsequent purchase ("Admiral-Avco VTR," 1970). In 1972 Avco's Cartridge TV, Inc. formed a joint venture with Columbia Pictures, called Cartridge Rental Network, in order to rent movies on its nonrewindable videotape for from three to six dollars per play ("Joint-Venture," 1972).

The advent of the Betamax in the United States spurred the next movement in the prerecorded tape market. In 1976 Time-Life Multimedia announced it would rent prerecorded Beta videocassettes via direct-mail distribution. Another New York-based company, Teletronics International, said it, too, was renting videocassettes directly to the consumer, charging a price comparable to a movie admission ("Prerecorded Programming," 1976).

It was not until October 1977, however, that the prerecorded video business in the United States was truly born. At that time, a Detroit-based entrepreneur named Andre Blay launched a direct-mail business called the Video Club of America. Blay had previously bought the rights from Twentieth Century Fox Film Corporation to sell fifty of its feature films on videotape for a total price of $500,000 a year plus a royalty of $7.50 on each cassette sold. Using the national magazine *TV Guide* as a primary media vehicle for reaching his prospective customers, Blay sold 250,000 cassettes by the end of the year (Lardner, 1987, pp. 173–174). Blay also utilized trade magazines to reach wholesalers and retailers and soon was supplying 300 to 400 of them with tapes. Owners of videocassette recorders now had a second use for their machines: watching first-run movies without having to tape them from broadcast television.

Within a month after the launch of Blay's mail-order video club, Betamax prerecorded tapes were being sold and rented at the retail level to the American public. Video store owners bought the cassettes from Blay or other entrepreneurs who had obtained video rights to films from other sources. Waleed Ali, a Chicago-based dealer, was another early pioneer who influenced the direction of the business. He bought videotapes of several hundred films from a distributor named Bill Blair, who had previously procured the video rights to 400 motion picture titles from a company called Gold Key. Blair then sold regional distributorships to local dealers, starting with Ali, who, in turn, sold the cassettes via mail order or to local retailers for either sale or rental. This was the beginning of a complex national distribution system that grew to a $2.6 billion market with sales in 1987 of 110 million videocassettes ("Home Video's Pioneers," 1987).

Among Andre Blay's first customers was a California businessman, George Atkinson, who is now generally credited as the first retailer to promote the rental, rather than the sale, of prerecorded videocassettes ("Home Video's Pioneers," 1987). Atkinson rented taped movies to customers for $10 a day from a 600-square foot store in West Los Angeles. He subsequently franchised his operation, helping other retailers to open video stores for which he supplied the videotape product (Lardner, 1987, p. 176).

Initially the motion picture studios were reluctant to license their films for distribution on videotape, but ultimately every major studio, including MCA/Universal (which was simultaneously suing Sony for copyright infringement), established a special videotape distribution unit (Lindsey, 1979a). At first, the studios were relatively sanguine about prerecorded videotape sales. They became less happy when they discovered video dealers were increasingly buying videotapes from them for rental purposes—for which the studios received no extra revenue—rather than for sale. The studios have tried a variety of plans to gain more effective financial control over the rental of their products, but none has worked so far. The conflict between the studios and the video dealers over the issue of revenue from rentals continues to be a contentious one with no resolution in view ("Home Video's Pioneers," 1987).

THE HOME VIDEOCASSETTE RECORDER COMES OF AGE IN THE UNITED STATES

In 1978 U.S. television-set manufacturers and marketers reported that they had sold 400,000 one-half-inch format videocassette recorders to dealers. This was the first year unit sales of videocassette recorders were reported as an industry category ("TV Makers Forecast," 1978). The previous year's unit sales had been estimated by the editors of *Television Digest* (the leading industry trade publication) to be 160,000 on the basis of U.S. government-supplied import data. These figures represented an increase of 151 percent from 1978 to 1979 ("VCR Growth," 1982).

While home videocassette recorder sales soared, Sony and its Betamax allies were waging a losing battle about the home video format as the VHS forces gradually began to dominate the U.S. consumer market. Each time Sony and its licensees marketed a new version of the Betamax with an extended playing time, the VHS marketers offered still more playing time ("VHS Gaining," 1978). In April 1979 Matsushita announced it was manufacturing VHS format videocassette recorders for the U.S. market with a recording capacity of six hours, bettering the Betamax's four-and-one-half-to-five-hour capability ("VHS's 3rd Speed," 1979). By July 1979, a Time magazine survey revealed VHS videocassette recorders outnumbered Betamax units by a ratio of seventy-one to twenty-eight ("VHS 71, Beta 28," 1979).

The rate of videocassette recorder sales in the United States slowed in 1979 (only an 18 percent increase over the previous year) but accelerated again in 1980. Sales increased from 475,000 units in 1979 to 805,000 units the following year ("Color TV Analogy," 1984). Aggressive competition, which saw retail prices reduced to less than $700 per unit, was considered to be a significant factor in this sales growth ("CES Sees Big," 1980).

However, about this time, the prerecorded industry also began to develop and raise the consciousness of the American public about a use for the videocassette recorder beyond the time-shifting concept that Sony's Akio Morita had originally perceived as the videocassette recorder's primary purpose. Recent movies were becoming readily available on videotape for only a few dollars a day at thousands of newly opened video rental stores throughout the United States.

The discounted price for videocassette recorders and the availability of relatively new films on tape combined to trigger a massive increase in the sales of videocassette recorders in 1981. With retail prices sliding down to about $500 per unit, sales increased more than 69 percent, resulting in 1,361,000 units sold to U.S. dealers. By the end of the year, videocassette recorders were in 26 percent of all U.S.

television households ("VCR Growth," 1982). The sales surge continued in 1982 as the competitive climate became more heated. A videocassette recorder could be purchased at a discount store for less than $400 and the Electronic Industries Association reported unit sales of 2,035,000 ("1982 Sales," 1983).

In addition to the heavily discounted prices and the availability of recent Hollywood films on videotape, the clamor of the opposing camps in the Betamax legal dispute—as they fought each other in the press and in the halls of Congress—was still fanning the U.S. public's awareness of the industry. Just prior to the January 1984 Supreme Court decision that legitimatized the right of Americans to videotape in their homes, the annual sales volume of videocassette recorders in the United States increased 101 percent. During 1983, a total of 4,091,000 units had been sold to U.S. dealers ("State of the Industry," 1984).

The Betamax format continued to lose ground to the VHS; its share of the market dropped to about 19 percent of the total videocassette recorders sold by dealers in 1983 ("VCR Share Survey," 1984), even though both Betamax and VHS models were selling for as little as $270 ("$250 VHS Coming?" 1984).

The Hollywood film studios, which had earned only $20 million (or 1 percent of their total income) from videotapes in 1980, had earned $625 million (or 14 percent of their total income) from them by the end of 1983. By 1987, videocassette sales had greater value to the studios than did theatrical exhibition of motion pictures (Scherick, 1987, p. 64).

The sale of home video rights had become a vital part of the studio's revenue base. The sixteen largest American videotape distributors, which include the top seven Hollywood studios, earned $1.9 billion in wholesale revenues on the 427 titles they released in 1988. The prerecorded video industry made $3.5 billion in 1987, contrasting starkly with the $1.9 billion earned by film theaters for the motion picture companies ("What's New," 1989). As an example of the value of home video to filmmakers, George Lucas' *The Empire Strikes Back* was sold to a home video distributor for $12 million ("The Competition," 1984).

At the close of 1984, the Electronic Industries Association reported 7,615,800 videocassette recorders had been sold to U.S. dealers that year, an increase of 86 percent over the previous year ("State of the Industry," 1985). As Korean-produced units came into the United States, bargain-hunting consumers could buy a machine for less than $200 ("January Street Prices," 1985). Sony finally began to retreat from the one-half-inch category. It announced it was preparing to launch a new 8mm videocassette recorder format, which it described as "the complete home video system of the future," adding it was intended to be the ultimate successor to the one-half-inch video format ("Sony Commits," 1985). Sony withdrew the Betamax from the U.S. market completely in 1986, replacing it with an improved one-half-inch format called Super Beta, as well as with the previously announced 8mm system ("First of 1987 Models," 1986).

In a repeat scenario of the original battle over format supremacy between Beta and VHS, JVC launched a direct attack on Sony's new 8mm technology, telling consumers through its advertising, "Don't Get Behind the 8 Ball" ("JVC Launches Attack," 1989). In response to Sony's thrust toward miniaturization of videocassette size, JVC countered by introducing VHS-C, a modified, but compatible, version of the VHS format. "With VHS-C," said Yoshihro Veno, managing director of JVC's Video Division, "consumers don't need another format to get smaller sized equipment."

There were 11.3 million videocassette recorders sold to U.S. dealers in 1985, an increase of 55.6 percent over the previous year's sales volume ("Official 1985 Sales Figures," 1986). In 1986 the Electronic Industries Association reported 13 million videocassette recorders were sold to dealers ("Slow Motion," 1987). (Table 6.1 shows the sales of videocassette recorders to dealer, retail prices, and percentage of penetration in U.S. TV homes 1975–1987.)

The U.S. sales volume of videocassette recorders began to slow down in 1987. This slowdown, according to industry analyst Paul Kagan, may have been caused by two factors: (1) the change of marketing focus toward homes with less disposable income because higher income homes had already acquired at least one videocassette recorder and (2) the competition from alternative electronic media forms (e.g., cable television, pay television, and pay-per-view), which might effectively challenge the videocassette recorder for a part of the consumer's dollar ("The VCR Future," 1987). Projections of the VCR's eventual penetration into American homes by the mid-1990s range from a conservative estimate of 75 percent to as much as 90 percent ("Drive-In Movies," 1988).

In January 1988 Sony announced it would begin selling videocassette recorders utilizing the VHS format. Twelve years after Sony successfully introduced its Betamax to the United States, its one-half-inch format accounted for only about 12 percent of the market. The vast majority of videocassette recorders being used in American homes were other manufacturers' versions of the rival VHS format ("Sony, in Shift from Beta MSX," 1988).

By May 1990, Alexander and Associates reported that VCRs were in more than 70 percent of all U.S. TV households, representing more than 61 million homes. The research anticipated VCRs being in more than 90 percent of U.S. TV homes by the mid-90s (VCR Penetration

Table 6.1
Videocassette Recorders, 1976–1987

Year	Sales to Dealers	Low End Retail Price
1976	55,000	$1,300
1977	160,000	1,100
1978	401,930	950
1979	475,000	895
1980	805,000	695
1981	1.4 million	500
1982	2.0 million	450
1983	4.0 million	400
1984	7.6 million	300
1985	11.3 million	250
1986	12.0 million	200
1987	11.7 million	200

Source: *Television Digest* estimates, 1976–1988.

Breaks 70%," 1990). A 1987 study Nielsen Media Research revealed that 14 percent of all prerecorded videotapes were being rented in U.S. drugstores and groceries, an increase of 9 percent from six months earlier ("Home Video Industry," 1988). There were 19,000 prerecorded titles available, an increase of 30 percent over the previous year. Video rentals increased from 1.1 billion in 1986 to 1.4 billion in 1987 ("Video Cassettes Pushing Books," 1988). By the end of 1987, the average rental rate of videotapes had reached $2.20 ("Paul Kagan's VCR Letter," 1988).

Retail sales and rentals of prerecorded videotapes were $9.2 billion. There were about 27,000 retail stores that specialized in selling or renting videos ("What's New," 1989). (Table 6.2 shows sales of prerecorded videocassettes to U.S. dealers 1980–1987.)

Since its practical development in the early 1950s, the videotape recorder has evolved from a complex, expensive mechanism with applications limited to the commercial broadcast field to a popular

Table 6.2
Sales of Prerecorded Videocassettes to U.S. Dealers (Excludes "Adult and Public Domain" Material)

Year End	Prerecorded Cassettes	% Increase Over Prior Year	% Increase 1987 Compared to
1987	110,000,000	+ 31.0	--
1986	84,000,000	+ 61.5	+ 31.0
1985	52,000,000	+136.4	+ 111.3
1984	22,000,000	+131.6	+ 400.0
1983	9,500,000	+ 58.3	+1,057.9
1982	6,000,000	+ 9.1	+1,733.3
1981	5,500,000	+ 83.3	+1,900.0
1980	3,000,000	--	+3,566.7

Source: Motion Picture Association of America, *U.S. Economic Review*, (1987), p. 9. Reprinted with permission of Motion Picture Association of America.

media technology that has given millions of people the ability to gain control of their own television viewing patterns. The videocassette recorder played a major role in producing a shift of consumer electronics research and development, as well as manufacturing, from the United States to the Far East and has contributed to the current foreign trade deficit crisis.

After an initial period of resistance, the motion picture industry has embraced the videocassette recorder as an important new source of revenue. Indeed, the videocassette recorder market has already successfully challenged film houses, becoming the most significant source of revenue in the movie distribution business. The videocassette recorder is still being watched warily by the broadcast television and advertising industries, which are not yet sure whether its pervasive position in American television households is a boon or a threat to their future prosperity.

However, there is little doubt that, as generations of technologically proficient consumers grow increasingly comfortable using the video-cassette recorder, the machine is likely to become a looming and po-tent presence in the American media environment. (Table 6.3 shows TV and VCR households and percent of VCR penetration 1975–1987.)

Table 6.3
VCR Households and Percent Penetration

	TV Households (000)	VCR Households (000)	% of TV Households
1975	68,500	--	--
1976	69,600	--	--
1977	71,200	--	--
1978	72,900	200	0.3
1979	74,500	400	0.5
1980	76,300	840	1.1
1981	79,900	1,440	1.8
1982	81,500	2,530	3.1
1983	83,300	4,580	5.5
1984	83,800	8,880	10.6
1985	84,900	17,600	20.8
1986	85,900	30,920	36.0
1987-mid-year	87,400	42,560	48.7
1987-year end	90,000	48,000	53.3(a)

Source: *Trends in VCR Usage*, Television Bureau of Advertising (TvB), (July 1987), p. 3. Reprinted with permission of Television Bureau of Advertising.
aThe *New York Times*, March 18, 1988, p. D4.

7

Videotape's Impact

The previous chapters have endeavored to show the evolution and adoption of videotape in the broadcast, nonbroadcast, and home video markets. In this chapter we shall attempt to bring the strands of the videotape story together in order to (1) determine what impact the videotape medium has had on various aspects of American culture within the "intellectual" contexts of such writers as Harold Innis, Marshall McLuhan, Neil Postman, Eric Havelock, and others, and (2) what the future for videotape may bring.

In Chapter 1, we presented eight general principles that lead to implications regarding the introduction and diffusion of a new technology into a culture. Now that we have outlined the videotape story in the broadcast, nonbroadcast, and home video markets, we can begin to draw some conclusions:

1. dominant media (technologies) create knowledge empires that ultimately go into disequilibrium; for example, the ascendancy of television as "the" medium for news (as opposed to print) is attributable to the advent of videotape together with the development of television technology in general.

2. technologies generally have a bias toward either time or space; videotape's characteristics give it a clear bias toward

transcending (or shifting) time *and* space. Programing on an enormous range of subjects can be easily transported on a global basis, using "time-shift" methodology and satellite-delivered technology to suspend a time and space bias.

3. technologies create total environments that are not necessarily definable by the content of the technology; videotape technology has helped create an electronic communications environment that is different from the former "print" dominated culture.

4. technologies create a demand for themselves; since its commercial introduction in 1956, the videotape medium has been responsible for the creation of a $20+ billion industry, split among the broadcast, home video, and nonbroadcast television market segments.

5. the diffusion of a technology into a culture takes time and the process is evolutionary; videotape did not just suddenly burst into a $20+ billion industry. It took a few decades. Also, if we look at the longer view in terms of technological developments, it is clear the adoption of videotape technology on a broad scale required several refinements to the basic technology.

6. a dominant technology creates organization changes in a culture; the popular acceptance of videotape caused significant changes in the structure of (a) the broadcast and non-broadcast industries (forcing other components of the culture to accept subordinate roles), and (b) the home video market (radically changing the way in which the film industry distributed its products). Videotape has created organizational changes in the communications industry in general and within the television industry itself. Witness the changes in the ownership of the major broadcast television networks and the shifts created by the home video market.

7. the practitioners of a technology evolve their models, or paradigms of how a technology should be applied; broadcasters initially perceived videotape as a means of overcoming the problems created in programing network television shows across multiple U.S. time zones. Later, they began to reposition the use of videotape as a cost-effective means of overcoming the limitations of live and filmed television production (an aspect immediately recognized by early adopters in the nonbroadcast market).

8. refinements of the technology refine the models of use on the part of the practitioners; the evolution of videotape technology, such as the introduction of lightweight, more portable videotape technology, caused practitioners to modify and refine the models of use in the broadcast, non-broadcast, and home video fields. The diffusion of videotape into American culture specifically, and Western *and* Eastern culture in general, certainly reflects some of the above observations.

Chapter 3 demonstrates that as the videotape medium became more widely adopted, particularly in the home video context, it produced significant economic and organizational changes in the television industry itself (in 1989 a $28 billion industry in terms of advertising sales), as well as in the culture at large. For example:

1. network television viewing patterns have been increasingly disrupted and modified since the mid-1970s (coincidental with the introduction of the one-half-inch Beta and VHS home video formats).

2. new electronic methods of delivering entertainment to U.S. television households was the primary cause of this disruption—e.g., advertiser supported cable television, pay television, and the home VCR—although nonaffiliated independent broadcast television stations' growth also contributed to the pattern of disruption (as well as the rise in ownership of privately owned satellite dishes in nonurban areas).

3. the television networks' policy of increasingly frequent commercial interruptions of programing (almost exclusively produced on videotape rather than film) caused the situation to deteriorate further).

This chapter also concluded that the viability of the mass audience concept for general interest television programing may be ending. It suggested that the future survival of the networks might depend on their ability to narrow the focus of their shows so that they would attract smaller but more desirable audiences (from the advertisers' viewpoint). It further suggested the likelihood that the three major television networks would be confronted by as many as two more networks in the future, further diminishing the entire industry's individual economic potential.

As evidence of this awareness, it was noted that all three networks have begun a process of diversification into alternative video mediums, such as cable TV and direct-to-home satellite networks and the production and distribution of prerecorded videotape.

Paralleling the adoption of videotape during the 1950s through the 1980s, the fragmentation of general interest audiences and loss of oligopolical control by the television networks is reflected in the conclusions of Chapter 4. In this chapter we observed:

1. during the late 1940s to 1959 sponsors assumed control of television programing, continuing the tradition begun in network radio. Single sponsorship of programs and advertising agency involvement in program development were also characteristic.

2. however, from 1960 to the mid-1980s the national television advertising community was forced to relinquish control of programing. Advertisers were compelled by the networks to start buying "scatter" or individual participations instead of continuing the tradition of single sponsorship of shows. During this period, advertisers began to seek greater efficiency for their network television investments by stressing the greatest amount of exposure of their advertising messages for each dollar they were spending. They also began to appreciate that not everyone in the television audience was equally valuable to them as existing or prospective customers, causing them to pursue more targeted audience segments.

3. from the early 1980s to the present, national television advertisers began reexamining their financial commitment to the three television networks, reallocating increasingly larger percentages of their total promotional budgets to other media in an attempt to more efficiently reach the audiences being lured away from network television by cable television, nonaffiliated television stations, and the home VCR.

4. advertisers are now expressing worry about the rising costs of network television advertising. They are also concerned about growing commercial "clutter" problems and commercial avoidance (zipping and zapping). Responding to that concern, advertisers and their agencies are beginning to package or produce their own wholly sponsored programing for delivery to the networks, as they did in earlier decades. They are also beginning to experiment with new forms of TV advertising which are designed to neutralize an increasing tendency toward the use of technological devices (like the fast forward capability of the VCR) to achieve commercial avoidance.

The $6 billion + (hardware and software) nonbroadcast television market (discussed in Chapter 5) is a market almost totally dependent on videotape technology for its existence. Even so, it too reflects some of the fragmentation, decentralization, and democratization characteristics that have characterized the broadcast/cable television market. In particular this chapter concluded that:

1. over the course of more than 30 years, videotape (as a communications medium) has permeated virtually all corporate and noncorporate institutions and departments within these organizations and affected both the internal and external audiences these organizations communicate with.

2. videotape—as an electronic communications technology— may be a contributing factor to the ostensible diminution of the authority of middle managers in many organizations, that is, with videotape top managers can have a direct line to other parts of the organization.

3. videotape has almost totally displaced 16mm film for both production and distribution purposes.

The $17 billion (hardware and software) home video market (see Chapter 6) would not exist if videotape technology had not been successfully introduced to the United States three-and-half decades ago. The home video market is similar to the nonbroadcast market in that its very existence is virtually dependent on the advent of videotape technology. Theoretically, the broadcast/cable TV industry could function without videotape technology. However, the same is largely not true of the nonbroadcast market and is absolutely certain regarding the home video market.

Even so, the conclusions of Chapter 6 again lead us to observe that the wide adoption of the videotape medium is concomitant with a fragmentation of audience. For example:

1. since its commercial introduction in 1956 the videotape recorder has evolved from a mechanism initially limited to the professional broadcast and nonbroadcast television fields to a popular technology that provides consumers with control over television viewing patterns within their homes.

2. the VCR played a major role in the redeployment of consumer electronics research and development and manufacturing activities from Western Europe and the United States to the Far East.

3. after first resisting the popular adoption of the technology, the American motion picture industry subsequently embraced the VCR as a primary source of revenue through its distribution of prerecorded feature films on videotape cassette.

4. the television and advertising industries are closely monitoring the development of the VCR. No consensus has yet been reached about whether it is a boon or a threat to their long-term economic survival. However, both industries have taken an accommodating posture in the short term. The television networks are currently encouraging the videotaping of their programs in the hope that audiences will time-shift them for viewing at a later time. Advertisers are aggressively seeking sponsorship opportunities of newly released Hollywood movies on prerecorded videotape in the hope of catching the attention of audiences who are now watching films on their VCRs instead of watching television. As of this writing, one of the highest rated TV shows on network television bases its programing content on viewers' submissions of their amateur home videos. Many local television news shows actively encourage their viewers to submit their home videos for airing.

5. the VCR is likely to become an ever-more important part of the U.S. media environment as new generations of increasingly technologically proficient consumers become even more comfortable with the technology. Reflecting this trend, several consumer electronics manufacturers are now offering prospective customers VCRs which can be programed by telephone to record television programs in their homes.

From Chapter 2, we found two factors upon which the diffusion of videotape technology depended: standardization and portability. To reiterate, following videotape's commercial introduction in 1956, the next most significant event took place in 1959 when the Society of Motion Picture and Television Engineers developed standards for the technology. Also in 1959 Toshiba demonstrated the one-head helical scan format which required a less speedy videotape transport, resulting in an overall less expensive machine and the potential for greater portability.

From these early developments in helical scan technology other developments followed, including the introduction of one-inch and one-half-inch helical scan reel-to-reel machines in the early to mid-1960s. Following this, Sony commercially introduced the three-quarter-inch

U-matic videocassette in 1971, a format which was more accessible than the one-inch and the one-half-inch reel-to-reel helical scan formats. This development allowed potential adopters even greater access to the technology.

The standardization issue was again relevant in the late 1960s when EIAJ standards were introduced for helical scan machines. The Japanese introduced even smaller helical scan formats (Beta and VHS) in the 1970s, making duplication and distribution even less expensive.

These technology developments provide evidence that there is a direct relationship between the introduction of a technology into a culture and its impact on that culture, as proposed by Innis, McLuhan, Havelock, and Postman.

As the videotape technology evolved, so did its use in the broadcast, nonbroadcast, and home video contexts.

As the technology became more accessible (standardized) from a user perspective, the number of adopters grew significantly.

The technology did indeed seem to have a bias toward space, as Innis would have contended.

In the nonbroadcast market context, videotape seemed to complement other media, rather than competing or becoming a dominant medium to the detriment of other media, with the exception of 16mm film, which appears to be on the wane as a primary communications tool.

As the videotape technology became more standardized, or accessible, top management in the nonbroadcast market became more involved in the use of the medium, on the one hand, and audiences at greater distances from corporate headquarters had opportunities to receive messages on videotape, on the other. Further, as the technology evolved, audiences tended to become more and more decentralized.

The physical viewing environments for videotaped presentations expanded as the technology evolved, consistent with McLuhan's beliefs, from programing originating at a broadcast station to programs originating and viewed at will in the home.

Videotape professionals' working paradigms evolved along with the technology, as Kuhn might have contended. Professionals moved from a central concern with the operation of the technology to a concern with content and style of presentation and use of programing at the point of viewing. In other words, as time went on, the technology became transparent.

The evidence indicates that within a few years of its commercial introduction, users had adopted the videotape medium for reasons and uses other than those originally intended. According to Erik Barnouw (1975) in *The Tube of Plenty*, in the early 1960s the videotape recorder made it easy for affiliate stations to tape a prime-time documentary and use it in a fringe period. Some stations, he said, made a habit of this (p. 384). In other words, even though the videotape medium was originally intended for use by broadcasters to "time delay" prime-time programs, corporations, for example, adopted the medium to transcend a problem in "space". The Udylite Corporation, for example, used videotape technology in 1959 to provide potential buyers with a video tour of their production facilities. In effect, the videotape presentation transcended space. Potential buyers could not go to the plant; the plant was brought to them in a way that was only one step removed from a live tour.

This is pure Harold Innis. Innis (1951a) contended:

A medium of communication has an important influence on the dissemination of knowledge over space and over time. According to its characteristics it may be better suited to the dissemination of knowledge . . . over space, than over time, particularly if the medium is light and easily transported. (p. 33)

Videotape in any of its helical scan formats (one-inch, one-half-inch reel-to-reel, three-quarter-inch videocassette, one-half-inch VHS and Beta) is "light and easily transported."

Innis' perception that "the character of the medium of communication tends to create a bias in civilization favourable to an overemphasis on the time concept or on the space concept" (ibid.) is also reflected in the reasons given by users of the videotape medium. Two reported reasons for the use of the medium in the nonbroadcast context (can reach decentralized audiences and extends the subject expert), for example, are clearly "space" biased reasons.

But users also mention several other reasons that are "time" oriented, although not time biased, that is, can manipulate real time-real life, saves time, fast turnaround from production to distribution. These reasons reflect a concern with transcending time, although not in the same sense as Innis might have articulated. Before 1971, non-broadcast users seemed more concerned with trainee participation; after 1971, users emphasized communications effectiveness—the impact of the medium once it gets to an audience.

The shift in reasons is a reflection of the advent of the videocassette in 1971. Prior to its introduction, it appears much use of the videotape medium was divided fairly evenly between centralized audiences and decentralized audiences. The applications, most of which were first reported before 1971, were heavily involved with training: sales training, skill training, role playing, as well as employee communications. The 1969 Stroh study corroborates that the major use of the medium was for training.

Training implies a direct relationship between trainers and trainees. It is conceivable the videotape medium (most likely, according to Stroh, the one-half-inch reel-to-reel format, a somewhat unwieldy but inexpensive format) was used extensively for training purposes. Much of this training was centralized. In other words, programs were not produced for distribution. Rather, they were produced for showing to trainees brought to some central or regional location. (In the case of role playing, the tape was instantaneously produced.)

Thus, the technology available prior to 1971 created a communications environment that did not support the wide distribution of videotape programing but rather fostered an environment that could be described as "centralized". In this context, users would naturally be more concerned with trainee participation because trainees were, more or less, face-to-face with the trainers (and the producers of videotaped training presentations).

After 1971 this changed. The videocassette created an ability to more effectively transcend space: programing could be produced in one location and get distributed cost-effectively to other locations, whether one or hundreds, whether domestic or international. With this shift, users and producers became separated from face-to-face contact with trainees. This seems to be reflected in the shift in reasons given by users; after 1971 users emphasized communications effectiveness, the impact of the medium once it gets to an audience, rather than trainee participation.

This may be evidence McLuhan is correct in his contention that media create total environments. Seemingly, after 1971 videotape technology becomes transparent and users are more concerned with the process of creating programing and the impact of the medium once the program gets to its intended audience. It appears users have moved to another level of response. After 1971 the technology has been transcended; it is "communications effectiveness" that counts, not "technological effectiveness".

Perhaps a comparison can be made to the advent of the videocassette in 1971 and movable type printing in 1455. Prior to movable type technology, the making of books was laborious; in Innisonian terms, Bible content was monopolized by the Church. Subsequent to the introduction of movable type, the Gutenberg printing press, there resulted a significant growth in the dissemination of facts, ideas, information, and knowledge. Once the technology of producing books in a more standardized, efficient way had been transcended—resulting in a speed-up in the dissemination of facts, ideas, information, and knowledge—people could more readily concern themselves with *new* facts, ideas, information, and knowledge. As Elizabeth L. Eisenstein (1983) states in *The Printing Revolution in Early Modern Europe*, "the new print technology made food for thought much more abundant and allowed mental energies to be more efficiently used" (p. 259).

In other words, when the technology of making books was slow and laborious, the content and ideas of these books tended to be time bound. The Gutenberg solution to this technological problem allowed the clock of knowledge to move forward. The Gutenberg printing press allowed facts, information, and knowledge to transcend space, resulting in the Renaissance, the Industrial Revolution, and ultimately the electronic age in which we live.

In contemporary terms, a comparison could be made between the typewriter (a descendent of the printing press) and the word processor (a descendent of the computer). The typewriter standardized handwriting. It is consistent, technically letter perfect. It is also linear. The word processor reflects all these characteristics, but adds more. The word processor also allows manipulation of content: you can move paragraphs at will. It can also check your spelling. The word processor allows the user to create several drafts of a letter, article, book or dissertation with great efficiency, once the original draft has been set. The word processor provides greater opportunities for content juxtaposition. It is the print counterpart to the graphics computer (which allows the user to visualize and analyze an object or concept from various points of view, separately or simultaneously). The speed of the manipulation of content with the word processor also is faster than that of the typewriter. It is the same difference between copying a Bible by hand and printing a Bible by press. The latter is faster, more efficient and more consistent in product output. It also results in the potential acceleration of content manipulation, which, in turn, results in the development of new points of view and perception, new ideas, the discovery of new facts, and new technologies.

McLuhan is explicit in his contentions regarding the advent of new technologies and other media. In *The Gutenberg Galaxy* (McLuhan, 1962), he states, "Technological environments are active processes that reshape people and other technologies alike" (p. 8). And in *Understanding Media* (McLuhan, 1964) he comments, "Today, with the cinema and the electronic speed-up of information movement, the formal structure of the printed word, as of mechanism in general stands forth like a branch washed up on the beach" (p. 174). Further on he posits, "A new medium never ceases to oppress the older media until it finds new shapes and positions for them" (ibid.).

These contentions can be readily seen in the three videotape markets previously discussed. For example, in the broadcast segment, videotape has totally replaced film as a "reporting" medium for news programing. A few exceptions include *60 Minutes* and various other magazine format news programs.

Videotape has virtually replaced film with respect to the airing of television commercials. While 35mm film is still used to shoot commercials, editing and distribution is universally accomplished on videotape.

Videotape has become a popular medium for the origination of certain kinds of programing. With the exception of such programs as *Dallas, Dynasty,* and *Wiseguy* a major portion of commercial television programing is originated, edited, and distributed on videotape.

In the nonbroadcast market it is clear 16mm film has been reduced in importance. What seems to have occurred is that with the advent of videotape, print, slides, and films were no longer the only communications options. Similar to the comparison of the typewriter and the word processor, the videotape medium could do things other media could not. The best early example is the role playing application. None of the other media can provide a user with instant replay, a characteristic essential to role playing training and inherent to the videotape medium.

Film's importance was also reduced in terms of audience size. Film is traditionally perceived as a large group gathering medium, in parallel with the experience of going to a movie theater. Videotape and the accessibility of three-quarter-inch and VHS distribution formats created the opportunity for smaller group gatherings, even gatherings of one person. In this sense McLuhan is correct: the new videotape medium (aesthetics aside) could do what film could do but also more; in effect, creating a new ratio among all the media in the nonbroadcast communications context.

In the home video market, film has also fallen on hard times. The video camcorder has totally replaced the super eight movie camera in American homes. Baby's first bath or the family backyard barbecue are now preserved on videotape not film. Even old home movies that had been previously recorded on film are now commonly transferred to videotape for purposes of preservation, or easier presentation on the television set in the family living room. The trend toward acceptance of the camcorder as the primary means of documenting significant family events in America has been stimulated by the increasing accessibility of lightweight 8mm camcorders which are rapidly replacing the VHS one-half-inch equipment as the American consumer's preferred format.

The wide adoption of the videotape medium has contributed to the modification of the oligopolistic character of the communications media landscape. In the broadcast television market, there were once only a few major players. With the advent of cable television and the growth of independent television stations, television audiences have significantly more choices. The prime-time audience for the so-called "Big 3" has been seduced by the large number of alternative programming choices that are now available. As a result, they have steadily abandoned their fiercely loyal commitment to viewing only network shows; choosing instead to flit across the channel spectrum giving dedicated loyalty to no single program source. These fickle tendencies have been further encouraged by a sense of liberation that viewers have come to experience as they become habituated to time-shifting programs on their VCRs—in essence becoming their own program directors.

Prior to videotape, television programing was dependent on the availability of television production facilities: the studio (and, in somewhat later years, remote origination facilities). With videotape, programing could be "put in the can" so to speak. With videotape, access to canned programing became as important, if not more important, as the ability to originate programing from a studio. Thus cable channels (such as the innovative HBO) could come into existence without a studio per se but with an access to feature film programing (distributed on videotape) and further distributed (ultimately) on a satellite channel. Light-weight and extremely portable camcorders could go into night-clubs to record live performances and deliver them with minimal post–production efforts to cable networks for transmission.

A parallel situation is observable in the nonbroadcast market. Users reported videotape was primarily a corporate staff management communications medium. And the vast majority of audiences for videotaped messages were highly select, whether the targeted audience was internal or external to the corporation.

These findings (for the nonbroadcast market segment) reflect directly and indirectly the monopoly theme articulated by Innis and McLuhan and the accessibility characteristic of media expressed by Havelock and Postman. After 1971, with the advent of the three-quarter-inch videocassette, videotaped messages grow more important on the organizational chart simultaneous to going out to more decentralized audiences (although overall videotape is used to communicate with select audiences, as opposed to general audiences).

The increased accessibility of the three-quarter-inch videocassette appears to be the cornerstone of the widespread diffusion of the medium in the corporate context. Once a format of the videotape medium appeared that was perceptibly easier to use—for production, editing, and especially distribution—than the former one-half-inch reel-to-reel formats, higher levels of management got into the act, so to speak, and broader distribution of videotaped messages was in evidence.

In effect, from its earliest uses (relevant to distribution), videotape was primarily used in centralized or regional areas: the distribution area for a program was constrained. Following the introduction of the three-quarter-inch videocassette, the distribution area of video-taped messages extended beyond centralized and regional areas to include all company locations, whether domestic or international. With the one-half-inch videocassette and growth of the home VCR market, companies extended their distribution of videotaped messages into the home.

If we liken the distribution history of videotape to a stone dropped into a pool, perhaps we can describe the diffusion of videotape technology in the early stages as the first ripple in the water, and in the later stages as the larger ripples. The same kind of analogy can be made in terms of the ascending use of the medium hierarchically before and after 1971, that is, before and after the advent of the three-quarter-inch videocassette. Before 1971, top management was conspicuous in its absence from its direct use of the medium. After 1971, this pattern was reversed. The presence of top management in videotaped messages to employees or external audiences seems almost concurrent with the introduction of the three-quarter-inch videocassette. Once a cost-efficient distribution medium was available, top management appears to have taken immediate advantage of it.

Top management's use of the videotape medium, particularly after 1971, implies a significant change in management style, organizational structure, and communications. Prior to 1971, with top management reportedly absent from the use of videotape as a communications med-ium, the typical organizational structure of the times—the hierarchical bureaucracy, based largely on a military/industrial model—was intact. Top managers were invisible. They remained in their boardrooms talk-ing among themselves. They communicated with their subordinates who, in turn, communicated corporate policies to subordinates, until ultimately orders were received by workers at the line level. Even the term "line management" implies a militaristic model. It is the kind of characteristic McLuhan might have dubbed "mechanistic". Innis might interpret this kind of organizational model as "monopolistic" in terms of the communications flow, that is, communication flows from the top of the organization down, until the workers at the bottom line of the so-called organizational chart get the message.

With videotaped messages, especially those in which top management appears, the typical hierarchical organization chart was implicitly subverted. Not only did top management become visible (even though it was not in the flesh), they were also communicating directly with line workers, in effect, subverting the bureaucratic authority (and communications monopoly) of middle managers.

. This is particularly reflected in the use of the medium for employee news. The vast majority of employee news programs are reportedly produced by workers not even in middle management; employees not that far from the bottom rung of the organizational chart. In many instances, these employees were choosing the content of employee news programs, providing higher level managers with an upward flow of information about employees and the company's operations that without videotape might have gone uncommunicated.

Overall, the videotape medium, based on the reports of users, seems to have contributed, by implication, to the creation of a communications environment that runs counter to the bureaucratic/militaristic hierarchy more typical of the post-World War II era. The videotape medium may have contributed to the creation of a communications flow that reordered the multilevel corporate organization to the potential detriment of middle management authority. The communications environment, therefore, became susceptible to being more holistic, open, and free-flowing, as opposed to the more rigid, closed, manual-oriented organization reflected in the bureaucratic/militaristic organizational hierarchy.

This raises the issues of accessibility, direction, and speed of information discussed by Postman. With the videocassette especially, both ends of the organizational chart gained access to the video medium on a larger scale after 1971. With the videocassette, the direction of management information communicated directly to various parts of the organization (as opposed to being distributed by middle levels of management) became like an exploding star. The videocassette also transcended the time it took to communicate information to various audiences.

The data also support Innis' contentions that new technologies have a bias toward either time or space. The videotape medium clearly is space biased to the extent that, just as satellites transcend the physical boundaries of nations, it transcends the organizational boundaries of departments, management levels, and programing distributors. Innis' contention that new technologies have the capacity to upend monopolies also seems to find support in the evidence. By implication, because the videotape medium can transcend organizational boundaries, it has the potential for breaking up the informational monopoly created by hierarchical conceptions of the corporate culture. In McLuhan's (1964) terms, videotape seems to be acting true to form: "Once a new technology comes into a social milieu it cannot cease to permeate that milieu until every institution is saturated" (p. 177).

As the evidence indicates, the videotape medium did not remain in the hands of a few television broadcasters, or producers, or in the trade show booth (à la Udylite), or in the role playing room, or in corporate conference rooms. To the contrary, the technology reached out beyond fixed (studio-bound) situations and gained access to various parts of the American culture through reduced cost of ownership and portability. The medium sought audiences beyond the confines of the physical studio. However, over time, and particularly with the advent of the videocassette format (which seemed to liberate the use of the medium for production, editing, and distribution), the medium was used for communicating to an ever-widening audience, in physical terms.

The process of videotape's inexorable march into every "milieu of the corporation" supports the contention that the medium sought the highest and broadest exposure: it was to be used for all manner of communications, by anyone and virtually every department in the organization, to a multitude of audiences, everywhere.

The evidence also lends support to Innis' economic emphasis. The technology chronology and the evidence found in the reported use of the videotape medium in the last thirty-four years clearly supports the position that as a medium declines in unit price (a factor in the law of supply and demand), so is there also a concomitant increase in the number of adopters.

The evidence also provides support for the crucial inherent need for standardization of a technology in order for its diffusion into a culture to occur at any meaningful level. This issue is discussed by McLuhan and Havelock. The evidence also highlights the need for portability for a meaningful level of diffusion to occur. Thus the evidence clearly indicates that a new technology does not merely burst into a culture and become diffused throughout. Certain things must happen first: the technology must become sufficiently standardized and portable for its widespread adoption.

The reported use of the videotape technology in American broadcast, nonbroadcast, and home video markets provides further evidence that, in McLuhan's (1964) words, "A new medium is never an addition to an old one, nor does it leave the old one in peace" (p. 174). In the context of this volume, the old medium is 16mm film, which, according to the evidence, appears to be almost nonexistent, having been largely replaced by videotape for both production, postproduction, and distribution.

Issues of accessibility to a technology, discussed by Postman, are also reflected in the evidence. The videotape medium, particularly after the 1971 introduction of the three-quarter-inch videocassette, gave access to television technology to both ends of the American corporate ladder: at the lower levels of the corporation, nontechnicians, with perhaps a few years of seniority, were given responsibility for producing corporate television programs; on the other end of the scale, top management reportedly began to use the medium for direct communication with lower and middle level employees. This reported use of the medium implies a significant shift in the direction of information flow in American corporations.

The same holds true for the broadcast and home video markets. Prior to 1971, only a very few consumers could afford to utilize videotape technology. Today, virtually anyone can buy the technology. In the broadcast market, videotape (together with developments in satellite and cable television technologies) has given access to commercial television audiences to many other entities beyond the original oligopolical CBS, NBC, and ABC television networks. HBO and other pay-TV cable networks now commonly package previously transmitted programing on videotape and market it to the public through retail video outlets. Other cable TV networks promote previously produced programs which have been repackaged on videotape directly to the viewer.

The previous chapters also provide evidence that as the medium evolved, so did user's paradigms evolve, as Kuhn would have contended. Thus, there is evidence to support the contentions of writers like Innis, McLuhan, Havelock, Kuhn, and Postman, namely: technologies have a bias toward either time or space; technologies create a demand for themselves; a technology creates organizational changes in a culture; the diffusion of a technology into a culture takes time and the process is evolutionary; and the practitioners of a particular technology evolve their models of how a technology should be applied and that refinements of the technology refine these models.

The material in the preceding chapters also lead to some other general conclusions about electronic technology in particular and the adoption of technology in general. For example, the experience of videotape's adoption in the broadcast, nonbroadcast, and home video markets appears to corroborate McLuhan's concept that electronic technology creates a "global village". In the nonbroadcast context, corporate managers can now communicate quickly with their employees and external audiences on a regional, national, and international level. (Seemingly paradoxically, the increasing use of satellite technology in professional nonbroadcast applications—so-called business television, a throwback to the days of live television—is helping to further increase the use of videotape). Geographically dispersed consumer activist groups exchange videocassettes to share knowledge and reinforce a sense of common purpose. The international system of pen pals may be soon replaced by "video pals".

The videotape experience appears to support Innis' contentions that media have a bias toward time or space. In videotape's instance the technology transcends space and therefore has a bias toward space. Further, Innis contended that as a medium declines in unit price, the number of adopters increase. This is certainly true in the case of the home VCR.

The history of the technology and the experience of the various markets that have adopted the videotape medium also lead to the conclusion that a technology must be sufficiently standardized and portable for it to be widely adopted. The advent of the three-quarter-inch videocassette in 1971 heralded its adoption in broadcast and non-broadcast professional markets; the introduction of the Beta and VHS formats in the mid-1970s certainly supports this conclusion. More recently, the increasing adoption of the 8mm format for consumers primarily interested in using their camcorders to record home movies further illustrates this point.

VIDEOTAPE'S FUTURE

Even a cursory analysis indicates videotape has a long way to go before it is obsolesced by another medium, if indeed it does become replaced, in the foreseeable future. Various communications environments are spurring the growth of videotape. For example, in 1972 a fledgling company called HBO started a cable channel that presented movies for pay; this was the beginning of pay cable television. Today there are dozens of satellite-delivered cable TV networks, both basic (advertiser supported) and pay, as well as pay-per-view networks offering first-run Hollywood movies. There are now approximately 6,500 cable television systems in the United States, some with public and commercial access channels. As channel capacity increases due to the introduction of fiber-optics, the cable TV environment will expand, together with the programing demands of the existing broadcast networks and nonaffiliated independent TV stations, further increasing the demand for programing via videotape.

The government regulatory environment is also helping to spur the growth of videotape. In 1982, the FCC gave the go-ahead for the establishment of Low Power Television stations (LPTV). This spawned the creation of several thousand new localized television stations, albeit with limited reach. These stations have a need for programing that is canned and inevitably is shown on videotape.

The home video market is spurring the growth of videotape. In 1981 there were only 3 million VCRs in American homes. By May 1989 61 million U.S. households had at least one VCR, representing a penetration level of almost 70 percent. This number is expected to increase within the next ten years to as much as 90 percent. Programing for VCRs is available on videotape.

The nonbroadcast market for videotape is also expected to expand the demand for videotape. According to the 1987 KIPI study (Stokes, 1988) the number of organizations using video technology for a variety of internal and external communications is projected to be 83,000 by 1995, an increase of 69.4 percent from 1987; a 204 percent increase since 1980!

The recent trend toward privatization of previously state-controlled television networks outside the United States has led to an enormous expansion of competitive stations, each relying almost entirely on videotape to produce and store their programing prior to transmission. Further, in many countries around the world, videos using news magazine formats are being sold to subscribers as a replacement for government controlled television news programs because of their skepticism about the shows' credibility. In many countries in the world where television programing is either not available or of an unappealing nature, citizens rely entirely on viewing prerecorded tapes of movies on their VCRs.

What about satellites and the video disc? The growth of satellite use will spur the growth of various kinds of teleconferencing (audio only, audio enhanced data, and video teleconferencing). But it is unlikely that in this decade teleconferencing will cause a displacement of the use of videotape. To the contrary, teleconferencing will probably provide communications opportunities that did not exist before, some of which will use videotaped programing as part of the presentation mix.

And the video disc? For a while it appeared as if the video disc could provide a challenge to videotape. But the performance of this new medium so far has been technically flawed. Production on video disc is costly and time consuming. Moreover, the ability to record and play back material immediately has not yet been commercialized, although it is technically possible. Several Japanese consumer electronics manufacturers showed prototype units at an industry trade show in Tokyo in the fall of 1989. However, manufacturers' commitment to videotape technology is large and ingrained. It is unlikely that within the 1990s the video disc will supplant videotape as a communications medium with any great meaning.

SPECULATIONS

Man's communications technologies have moved from the purely verbal (e.g., grunts and cries), to the alphabetic (as in Greek), the graphic (as in Gutenberg and painting), the filmic (as in photography), and currently to the electronic (as in videotape, television, radio, et al.). We have speculated that the video disc or some kind of laser/optical/digital device will ultimately supplant videotape as a primary means of recording and transmitting electronic information. But what is next? Since we have moved from the verbal, to the alphabetic, the graphic, the filmic, and the electronic, it would be absurd to presume that electronic is the end of the communications technology chain.

It is the essence of nature that nothing remains the same. The universe is in continuous motion, as are the galaxies, the stars, our solar system. Motion is constant—our planet around the sun, the moon around the earth, the weather, the continental plates, the forces of human history. It stands to reason that sometime in the future, perhaps in our lifetime, we will develop a new medium that is one step further advanced from the electronic. It is our opinion that the next significant medium will be based in some form on light. This "light" communications technology will be supported in some way by superconductivity technology. We already have some of the technological pieces in place, so to speak: laser technology, digital technology, superconductivity technology.

There is other evidence of a new communications technology on the horizon in the works of film producers, such as Gene Roddenberry and Steven Spielberg. *Star Trek*, for example, is full of light-based technologies: phasers, photon torpedoes, and the transporter. Steven Spielberg's *Close Encounters of the Third Kind* is a cornucopia of light. In fact the entire film is a parade of filmic expression based on the theme of light. In some way the development of the next generation of communications technology will be based on videotape. And this is *not* to say that videotape will vanish from the face of the earth as a significant communications technology at some future point. The history of technology is very much like a cross section of the Grand Canyon. Each bottom layer supports the layers on top; it is, thus, the nature of new technology to be additive. Each successive technology adds a new capability to the culture without necessarily doing away with the technological antecedent. If the reverse were true, we would have given up talking, reading and writing, printing and filming long ago.

The story of videotape is thus also the story of many technologies. Initial models are inevitably crudely engineered and expensive. As the technology is modified and becomes increasingly standardized and portable, its adoption increases throughout the culture. Ultimately, the technology spawns and evolves newer technology. It is a pattern observable in many other technologies (if not all). It is a pattern observable in cultures, in nations, in communities, in families, in individuals. It is the pattern of the universe, perhaps: growth and change is inexorable. Nothing stays the same forever.

Bibliography

Abramson, A. (1955). A short history of television recording. *Journal of the SMPTE, 64,* 250–54.

——— . (1973). A short history of television recording: Part II. *Journal of the SMPTE, 82,* 188–198.

A. C. Nielsen Media Research Television Audience Report. (1964–1986).

A. C. Nielsen Media Research Television Audience Report. (1987, 1988). Personal communication with authors.

Adams, V. (1956, April 15). TV is put on tape by new recorder. *New York Times,* pp. 1, 76.

Ad growth edges up. (1987, September 24). *Advertising Age,* pp. 1–2, 166.

Ad spending on TV rises. (1989, March 1). *New York Times,* p. D8.

Adler, R. P. (1981). *Understanding television: Essays on television as a social and cultural force.* New York: Praeger Publishers.

Admiral-Avco VTR. (1970, June 1). *Television Digest,* p. 11.

Advertisers cut spending pace. (1986, September 4). *Advertising Age,* pp. 1–2, 122.

Advertisers get into the act. (1989, October 9). *Broadcasting,* p. 50.

Agnew, C. M. & O'Brien, N. (1958). *Television advertising.* New York: McGraw Hill.

Agnew's blast only one of many in 1969. (1969, December 29). *Broadcasting* (Special Report), pp. 17–20.

Airline TV off the ground. (1964, July 6). *Television Digest,* p. 4.

Ampex and Toshiba will form joint manufacturing firm. (1964, February 3). *Television Digest,* p. 6.

ARB nationwide sampling sweep. (1969, February 24). *Television Digest*, p. 1.

Arvida turns to video to sell Florida project. (1988, March 3). *New York Times*, p. D4.

Atwan, R., Orton, B., & Vesterman, W. (1978). *American mass media: Industries and issues* (2d ed.). New York: Random House.

Back, G. L. (1979). The consequences of the Federal Communications Commission's prime-time access rule. *Dissertation Abstracts International*, *40*, 3601A. (University Microfilms No. 79–25,254)

Bar/LNA multi-media service report. (1987, January–September). (Available from Broadcasters Advertisers Report, 142 West 57th Street, New York, New York).

Barnouw, E. (1966–1970). *A history of broadcasting* (Vols. 1–3). New York: Oxford University Press.

————. (1975). *The tube of plenty*. New York: Oxford University Press.

————. (1978). *The sponsor: Notes on a modern potentate*. New York: Oxford University Press.

Barry, R. V. (1977). *Media use in nationally selected high school programs: A questionnaire survey of secondary school principals, English Department chairmen, and English teachers*. Ph.D. dissertation, Teachers College, Columbia University, New York.

Bartlow, L. (1970, August). CCTV at Illinois Bell. *Educational and Industrial Television*, p. 18.

Barzun, J., & Graff, H. F. (1957). *The modern researcher* (rev. ed.). New York: Harcourt, Brace, & World, Inc.

Bates bullies nets over VCR erosion. (1986, August 11). *Advertising Age*, p. 1.

Battle lines form as MCA sues industry. (1981, November 16). *Television Digest*, p. 9.

Bauer, D. E. (1971). *Current practices in the use of selected instructional media in the teaching of business subjects with implications for teacher education*. Ph.D dissertation, University of Nebraska, Lincoln.

BBDO. (1986). *Prime time: 1986–87*. New York: Author.

Behind Sony–Paramount home video deal. (1976, August 9). *Television Digest*, pp. 9–10.

Bennett, J. (1980, October 3). Video tape helps create and record twenty-five years of history. *3M Company*, pp. 1–12.

Bergreen, L. (1980). *Look now, pay later*. Garden City, NY: Doubleday & Company.

Big network expected to focus on cable TV. (1980, June 11). *New York Times*, p. 15.

Birth of a new era in TV technology. (1956, April 21). *Television Digest*, p. 1.

Birth of a new medium—Home video recording. (1966, August 1). *Television Digest*, p. 9.

Blumler, J. (1986). *Television in the United States: Funding sources and programing consequences/research on the range and quality of broadcasting services: A report for the Committee on Refinancing the BBE* (ISBN No. 0 11 34083 1).

Bogart, L. (1972). *The age of television: A study of viewing habits and the impact of television on American life.* New York: Frederick Ungar Publishing Company.

Booher, D. (1986). *Cutting paperwork in the corporate culture.* New York: Facts on File Publications.

British-made Wesgrove video tape recorder put on U.S. market. (1965, May 3). *Television Digest,* p. 9.

A broadcast history: 30th anniversary issue. (1983, November 21). *Television/Radio Age,* pp. 23–25.

Brooks, T., & Marsh, E. (1985). *The complete directory to prime-time network TV shows: 1946–present.* New York: Ballantine Books.

Brown, C. R. (1972). *Assessment of television and videotape recording for utilization in continuing medical education.* Ph.D. dissertation, Ohio State University, Columbus.

Brown, L. (1971). *Television: The business behind the box.* New York: Harcourt, Brace, Jovanovich.

———. (1977). *Les Brown's encyclopedia of television* (2d ed.). New York: New York Zoetrope.

———. (1979). *Keeping your eye on television.* New York: The Pilgrim Press.

Brown, L., & Walker, S. W. (Eds.). (1983). *Fast forward: The new television and American society.* Kansas City: Andrews & McMeel, Inc.

Brush, J. M., & Brush, D. P. (1974). *Private television: A report to management.* White Plains, NY: Knowledge Industry Publications.

———. (1977). *Private television communications: An awakening giant.* New Providence: International Television Association.

———. (1981). *Private television communications: Into the eighties (the third Brush report).* New Providence: International Television Association.

———. (1986). *Private television communications: The new directions (the fourth Brush report).* New York: HI Press.

———. (1988). *Private television communications: the fourth Brush report, update '88.* LaGrangeville, NY: HI Press.

Bunyon, J. A., Grummond, F. C., & Watson, N. A. (1978). *Practical video: The manager's guide to applications.* White Plains, NY: Knowledge Industry Publications.

Bureau of the Census. (1987). *Statistical abstracts of the United States.* Washington, DC: Government Printing Office.

Cable and ad agencies pow-wow. (1979, August 20). *Television Digest,* p. 3.

Cable: Billion-dollar baby. (1987, October). *Washington Journalism Review,* p. 10.

Cable eroding network's ad share. (1986, December 15). *Insight,* p. 46.

Cable TV ad sales soaring. (1987, November 9). *Advertising Age,* p. 2.

Carlson, R. P. (1971). *Utilization of newer instructional media by professional physical education faculty in teaching undergraduate majors at big ten universities.* Ph.D. dissertation, Indiana University, Bloomington.

Carpenter, E., & McLuhan, M. (1960). *Explorations in communication.* Toronto: Beacon Press.

Carter, R. (1966, January). Face-to-face communications. *Training in Business and Industry*, p. 38.

Cartridge TV halts production. (1973, July 9). *Television Digest*, p. 7.

CBS out, Polaroid in videoplayers. (1971, December 27). *Television Digest*, p. 6.

CBS's EVR launching—Its significance. (1968, December 16). *Television Digest*, p. 9.

CES sees big VCR price break. (1980, January 14). *Television Digest*, p. 7.

The changing picture in video tape for 1959–1960 (1959, 2d ed.). St. Paul, MN: Minnesota Mining and Manufacturing Company.

Chase Manhattan Bank in NYC scheduled conference on television house organs. (1973, June 11). *ETV Newsletter*, p. 3.

Chrysler-brand media spending is shifted to print. (1989, October 9). *Wall Street Journal*, p. B5.

Color EVR in fall at "B & W Price." (1970, March 30). *Television Digest*, p. 7.

Color TV analogy indicates VCR plateau. (1984, February 6). *Television Digest*, p. 15.

The competition looks on. (1984, December 24). *Time*, p. 53.

Copyright suit challenge, Beta sales. (1976, November 15). *Television Digest*, p. 7.

Corporate television news survey. (1978). International Television Association.

Courses by videotape. (1968, January 2). *Television Digest*, p. 3.

Czitrom, D. J. (1982). *Media and the American mind: from Morse to McLuhan.* Chapel Hill: The University of North Carolina Press.

"Daily viewing drops," says Nielsen. (1989, May 22). *Broadcasting*, p. 33.

DeLuca, S. M. (1980). *Television's transformation: The next twenty-five years.* San Diego: A. S. Barnes & Company, Inc.

de Sola Pool, I. (1983). What ferment? A challenge for empirical research. *Journal of Communications, 33*, 258–261.

Diamond, E. (1982). *SIGN OFF: the last days of television.* Cambridge, MA: The MIT Press.

DiscoVision closely resembles Philips VLP. (1972, December 18). *Television Digest*, p. 7.

Disk system loses at RCA. (1982, March 9). *New York Times*, sec. 4, p. 4.

Dobrow, J. R. (1987). The social and cultural implications of the VCR: How VCR use concentrates and diversifies viewing. *Dissertation Abstracts International, 48*, 500A. (University Microfilms No. 87–14,028).

Donnelly, W. J. (1986). *The confetti generation.* New York: Henry Holt & Company.

Dranov, P., Moore, L., & Hickey, A. (1980). *Video in the 80's,* White Plains, NY: Knowledge Industry Publications.

Drive-in movies. (1988, February). *Inc.*, p. 42.

Eisenstein, E. (1979). *The printing press as an agent of change: Communications and cultural transformations in early modern Europe* (Vols. 1–2). Cambridge: Cambridge University Press.

———. (1983). *The printing revolution in early modern Europe.* Cambridge: Cambridge University Press.

Ellul, J. (1962). The technological order. *Technology and Culture, 3*, 412–41.

————— . (1964). *The technological society* (J. Wilkinson, Trans). New York: Vintage Books.

Employee news video conference in New York, June 12. (1974, April 29). *ETV Newsletter*, p. 4.

Fairchild home video television hailed. (1964, April 20). *Television Digest*, p. 7.

Feder, B. J. (1981, October 20). Private videotaping of copyrighted TV rule infringement. *New York Times*, sec. 1, p. 1.

First home VTR deck on U.S. market. (1976, February 16). *Television Digest*, p. 9.

First of 1987 models from Sony. (1986, April 17). *Television Digest*, p. 10.

For radio-TV: Big year in the bag. (1966, February 21). *Broadcasting*, pp. 40, 42–48.

Forty-three years of tape progress. (1977, May 27). *Backstage*, p. 20.

Fox, S. (1984). *The mirror makers: A history of American advertising and its creators*. New York: William Morrow & Company.

Freeman, R. R. (1973). *Special education teachers' perception in regard to use and availability of media, Los Angeles Unified School District*. Ph.D. dissertation, Brigham Young University, Provo.

Futurists describe '80s to BFM. (1979, September 24). *Television Digest*, p. 5.

Gerbner, G. (1986). Living with television: The dynamics of the cultivation process. In J. Bryant & D. Zillman (Eds.), *Perspectives on media effects* (pp. 4–5). Hillsdale, NJ: Lawrence Erlbaum Associates.

Gerson, B. (1981, January). Happy birthday videotape! *Video Review*, pp. 54–55.

Getting a fix on how they're using all those VCR's. (1984, May 7). *Broadcasting*, pp. 74–75.

Gimpel, J. (1976). *The medieval machine: The industrial revolution of the middle ages*. Middlesex: Penguin Books.

Ginsburg, C. P. (1981). *The birth of video recording*. Presented in slightly different form at the 82nd convention of the Society of Motion Picture and Television Engineers. Reprinted: Redwood City, CA: Ampex Corporation, Audio-Video Systems Division. (Original work published 1957).

Glossary of home video terms. (1966, October 22). *Variety*, pp. 271, 275.

Gold, B. (1981, March). Technological diffusion in industry. *Journal of Industrial Economics*, pp. 247–69.

Goldstein, F., & Goldstein, S. (1983). *Prime-time television: A pictorial history from Milton Berle to Falcon Crest*. New York: Crown Publishers.

Gould, J. (1956, April 22). Taped television: Commercial use of new device offers great possibilities and problems. *New York Times*, p. 13.

Greenhouse, L. (1984, January 18). Television taping at home is upheld by the Supreme Court. *New York Times*, sec. 1, p. 1.

Hall, J. (1975, October). But first, this flushot reminder. *TV Guide*, pp. 24–25.

Happy 25th birthday to video tape (n.d.). St. Paul, MN: 3M Company, Magnetic Audio/Video Products Division.

Havelock, E. A. (1976). *Origins of western literacy*. Toronto: The Ontario Institute for Studies in Education.

Head, S., & Sterling, C. H. (1982). *Broadcasting in America: A survey of television, radio, and new technologies* (4th ed.). Boston: Houghton Mifflin.

————. (1987). *Broadcasting in America: A survey of electronic media* (5th ed.). Boston: Houghton Mifflin.

Heighton, E. J., and Cunningham, D. R. (1976). *Advertising in the broadcast media.* Belmont, CA: Wadsworth Publishing Company, Inc.

Hickey, N. (1982). *Television in transition.* Radnor, PA: Triangle Publications, Inc.

————. (1988, March 19–25). The verdict on VCRs (so far). *TV Guide*, pp. 12–14.

Holsti, O. R. (1969). *Content analysis for the social sciences and humanities.* Reading: Addison-Wesley Publishing Company.

Home tape study cues web grins. (1985, December 11). *Variety*, p. 78.

Home video industry feeling middle age. (1988, February 2). *New York Times*, sec. C, p. 15.

Home video recorders ruled lawful by judge. (1979, October 3). *New York Times*, sec. 4, p. 1.

Home video recording at slow speed. (1964, February 10). *Television Digest*, p. 7.

Home video recording at thirty IPS. (1964, June 8). *Television Digest*, pp. 8–9.

Home video's pioneers: In their own words. (1987, August 17–21). *Twice*, pp. 32–33.

Home VTRs under fifteen brand names. (1977, June 27). *Television Digest*, p. 8.

How people use VCRs. (1979, March 12). *Television Digest*, p. 11.

Hughes, E. H., & Musselman, V. A. (1969). *Introduction to modern business.* Englewood Cliffs, NJ: Prentice-Hall.

Innis, H. (1950). *Empire and communication.* Toronto: University of Toronto Press.

————. (1951a) *The bias of communication.* Toronto: University of Toronto Press.

————. (1951b). *Empire and communication* (7th ed.). Oxford: Clarendon Press.

Jackes, F. D. (1972). *The positive image: The federal government's use of motion pictures, 1901–1940.* Ph.D. dissertation, University of Pennsylvania, Philadelphia.

January street prices. (1985, February 4). *Television Digest*, p. 11.

Japan moves into technology lead. (1977, March 14). *Television Digest*, p. 9.

Joint-venture cartrivision program network. (1972, May 1). *Television Digest*, p. 10.

JVC launches attack on Sony 8mm (1989, June 19–23). *Twice*, p. 1.

JVC to market two-hour home VTR next month. (1976, September 13). *Television Digest*, p. 8.

Kuhn, T. S. (1962). *The structure of scientific revolutions.* Chicago: The University of Chicago Press.

Lardner, J. (1987). *Fast forward: Hollywood, the Japanese and the VCR wars.* New York: W. W. Norton & Company.

Lawsuit attacks sales of gear for home taping of TV. (1976, November 13). *New York Times*, sec. 1, p. 8.

Levy, M. (1981). Home video recorders and time shifting. *Journalism Quarterly, 58*, 401–405.

Lindsay, H. (1977, December; 1978, January). Magnetic recording part I and part II. Reprinted from *dB the Sound Engineering Magazine*, pp. 38–44; 40–44.

Lindsey, R. (1979a, July 2). Hollywood moves to tape video market. *New York Times*, sec. 3, p. 11.

———. (1979b, October 3). Home video recorders ruled lawful by judge. *New York Times*, sec. 3, p. 11.

Long, M. (1985). *1985 world satellite almanac: The complete guide to satellite transmission and technology.* Boise, ID: CommTek Publishing Company.

Long, S. L. (1979). *The development of the television network oligopoly.* New York: Arno Press.

Lyons, N. (1976). *The Sony vision.* New York: Crown.

Magnavox, Sylvania choose four-hour VHS. (1977, May 30). *Television Digest*, p. 7.

The marvels of magnetic tape. (1954, January). *Megaphone*, pp. 10–11.

McCabe, E. (1971, October). The video cassette: 1928–1971. *Training in Business and Industry*, pp. 43–55.

McLuhan, M. (1960a). Classroom without walls. In E. Carpenter & M. McLuhan (Eds.), *Exploration in communication* (pp. 1–3). Toronto: Beacon Press.

———. (1960b). The effect of the printed book on language. In E. Carpenter & M. McLuhan (Eds.), *Exploration in communication* (pp. 125–135). Toronto: Beacon Press.

———. (1962). *The Gutenberg galaxy.* Toronto: University of Toronto Press.

———. (1964). *Understanding media: The extensions of man.* New York: McGraw-Hill.

McLuhan, M., & Fiore, Q. (1967). *The medium is the massage.* New York: Bantam Books, Inc.

McLuhan, M., & Logan, R. K. (1977, December). Alphabet, mother of invention. *Et Cetera*, pp. 375–383.

Morgenthaler, E. (1974). Some firms like it if their employees watch TV at work. *Wall Street Journal*, pp. 1, 22.

Morita, A., with Reingold, E. M., & Shimomura, M. (1986). *Made in Japan.* New York: E. P. Dutton.

Motion Picture Association of America. (1987). *U.S. economic review.* Washington, DC: Author.

Movie videos are increasingly offering viewers more to watch—Commercials. (1988, March 29). *Wall Street Journal*, p. 33.

Mullin, J. T. (1976, April). Creating the craft of tape recording. *High Fidelity*, pp. 62–67.

Mumford, L. (1934). *Technics and civilization.* New York: Harcourt, Brace, & World, Inc.

Myrowitz, J. (1985). *No sense of place.* New York: Oxford University Press.

National Association of Broadcasters. (1967). *Standard definitions of broadcast research terms.* New York: Author.

National Association of Broadcasters. (1980). *Home video recorders: Some additional findings*. Washington, DC: Author.

National Cable Television Association document (1986, December).

Nayak, R. P., & Ketteringham, J. M. (1986). *Breakthroughs*. New York: Rawson Associates.

NBC on technology. (1979, February 20). *Television Digest*, p. 5.

NBC's aggressive foreign agenda is crimped by rules here and there. (1989, August 14). *Cablevision*, pp. 76–78.

Network-cable alliances in work. (1988, January 25). *Broadcasting*, p. 43.

Networks push program tie-ins for ads. (1988, October 24). *Wall Street Journal*, p. B.1.

Networks unconcerned about VCR. (1977, November 11), *Television Digest*, p. 8.

New channel for learning. (1960, 3rd Quarter). *Tartan*, pp. 8–9.

New Nielsen VCR data: The mystery of the vanishing audience revealed. (1985, November 4). *ADWEEK*, pp. 1, 6.

A new spin on videodiscs. (1989, June 5). *Newsweek*, p. 68.

New TV ratings device registers fewer viewers of network shows (1987, December 24). *New York times*, p. 1.

New universe of network TV calls for junking outworn ideas. (1988, January 20). *Variety*, p. 181.

1964 record: Best yet for both media (1965, February 22). *Broadcasting*, p. 78.

1982 sales. (1983, January 17). *Television Digest*, p. 13.

Novak, P. E. (1979). *A survey of media utilization in accredited associate degree nursing program administered by public community college*. Ph.D. dissertation, Southern Illinois University, Carbondale.

Official 1985 sales figures. (1986, January 20). *Television Digest*, p. 9.

100 leaders hit $13 billion mark. (1981, September 10). *Advertising Age*, pp. 1, 58, 98.

Ong, W. J. (1982). *Orality and literacy: The technologizing of the word*. London: Methuen & Company.

Outlook for telcan is clouded. (1964, August 6). *Television Digest*, p. 7.

P & G cut $75 million from network TV. (1988, February 22). *Advertising Age*, pp. 1, 73.

(Pat) Weaver is . . . hot about home video tape. (1964, December 7). *Television Digest*, p. 5.

Paul Kagan's VCR Letter, no. 33. (1988, March 8).

Philips VLP makes impressive debut. (1972, September 11). *Television Digest*, p. 8.

Phillips, L. W. (1981). Assessing measurement error in key informant reports: A methodological note on organizational analysis in marketing. *Journal of Marketing Research, 18*, 396.

Plan seen for another TV network. (1989, October 20). *New York Times*, p. D1.

Playtape and Avco in VTR venture. (1969, June 2). *Television Digest*, p. 6.

Poltz, R. G. (1981). *Communication in contemporary organizations*. In C. Reuss & D. Silvis (Eds.), *Inside organizational communication* (pp. 5–16). New York: Longman.

Postman, N. J. (1973, December). Media ecology: A growing perspective. *Media Ecology Review.*

———. (1979, Fall). The information environment. *Et Cetera*, pp. 234–245.

———. (1985). *Amusing ourselves to death.* New York: Viking.

Prerecorded programing for Betamax. (1976, February 23). *Television Digest*, p. 8.

Private videotaping of copyrighted TV rule infringement. (1981, October 20). *New York Times*, sec. 1, p. 1.

RCA's home VTR decision—What it means. (1977, April 4). *TV Digest*, p. 12.

RCA's SelectaVision—Home video phono. (1969, October 6). *Television Digest*, p. 7.

Reel, A. F. (1979). *The networks: How they stole the show.* New York: Charles Scribner's Sons.

Rogers, E. M. (1976, March). New product adoption and diffusion. *The Journal of Consumer Research*, pp. 290–301.

Roizen, J. (1976, January-February). Shoenberg Memorial Lecture, Royal Institution. Printed in *Television: Journal of the Royal Television Society*. pp. 15–21. (Original work published 1975, December 11).

Sanyo home VTR competes with Betamax. (1976, May 3). *Television Digest*, p. 9.

Scherick, E. J. (1987, November). Crossed circuits. *American Film*, pp. 63–64.

Schubin, M. (1976, July). One man's history of television. *Videography*, p. 55.

———. (1986, July). One man's history of television. *Videography*, pp. 49–50.

Schwartz, T. (1973). *The responsive chord.* Garden City: Anchor Press.

Sears, Ward embrace CartriVision. (1971, July 5). *Television Digest*, p. 8.

Sellers, P. (1988, March 14). Lessons from TV's new bosses. *Fortune*, pp. 115, 122.

Senate hearings this week on taping bills. (1981, November 30). *Television Digest*, p. 7.

Sherman, R. K. (1987, October/November). Zapping + zipping = big trouble. *BPME Image Magazine*, p. 30.

Slow motion for VCRs. (1987, May 24). *New York Times*, sec. 3, p. 1.

Smith Kline & French to run seminars on how it uses CCTV for employee communications. (1973, March 19). *ETV Newsletter*, p. 4.

Sony commits to 8mm as successor to one-half-inch VCR. (1985, April 22). *Television Digest*, p. 11.

Sony enters video player race. (1969, November 24). *Television Digest*, p. 8.

Sony HVR–Japan now, United States this year. (1975, April 21). *Television Digest*, p. 11.

Sony, in shift from Betamax, will sell rival VCR system. (1988, January 12). *New York Times*, pp. 1, D4.

Sony launches home video tape recording marketing. (1965, June 14). *Television Digest*, p. 11.

Sony 1980—Return to elegance. (1979, April 30). *Television Digest*, p. 7.

State of the industry. (1984, January 23). *Television Digest*, p. 14.

State of the industry. (1985, January 14). *Television Digest*, p. 10.

Stephens, R. E. (1971). *Factors in media utilization in higher education*. Ph.D. dissertation, University of Southern California, Los Angeles.

Sterling, C. H. (1984). *Electronic media: A guide to trends in broadcasting and new technologies 1920–1983*. New York: Praeger.

Sterling, C. H., & Haight, T. R. (1978). *The mass media: Aspen Institute guide to communication industry trends*. New York: Praeger.

Sterling, C. H., & Kittross, J. M. (1978). *Stay tuned: A concise history of American broadcasting*. Belmont, CA: Wadsworth.

Stokes, J. T. (1988). *The business of nonbroadcast television*. White Plains, NY: Knowledge Industry Publications.

Stop-Beta move shapes up in Japan. (1976, July 26). *Television Digest*, p. 8.

Stroh, T. F. (1969). *The use of video tape in training and development*. New York: American Management Association.

Suddenly, basic cable is offering more than basic fare. (1988, March 3). *Business Week*, p. 36.

Tape-it-yourself TV. (1965, September 17). *Life*, p. 57.

Tape that takes pictures. (n.d.). Release no. A8–25. Exclusive to Bill Stocklin, Radio Television News, 3M Company, St. Paul, MN, Product News, p. 1.

Teece, D. J. (1980, May). The diffusion of an administrative innovation. *Management Science, 26*.

Television Bureau of Advertising. (1987a). *Trends in Cable TV*. New York: Author.

———— . (1987b) *Trends in television*. New York: Author.

———— . (1987c). *Trends in VCR usage*. New York: Author.

———— . (1987d). *Trends in viewing*. New York: Author.

Television Digest. (1982, February 1). p. 13.

Television: No great upswing this year. (1968, January 29). *Broadcasting*, pp. 38–42, 44–46.

Ten years of video tape recording. (1966, May). *Industrial Electronics*, pp. 228–230.

They're watching more. (1973, January 1). *Broadcasting*, p. 15.

Thompson, T. (1980). *Organizational TV news*. Philadelphia: Media Concepts Press.

Toffler, A. (1970). *Future shock*. New York: Bantam Books.

———— . (1981). *The third wave*. New York: Bantam Books.

Top 100 advertisers hike total to $6.3 billion. (1976, August 23). *Advertising Age*, pp. 1, 74, 90.

Top 100 national advertisers hike ad total to $5.68 billion. (1974, August 26). *Advertising Age*, pp. 1, 38, 102.

Top 125 national advertisers put record $4.83 billion in promotion. (1969, August 25). *Advertising Age*, pp. 1, 42, 76.

Top 125 national advertisers spent $3.8 billion on ads, promotion. (1965, August 30). *Advertising Age*, pp. 1, 66, 88.

Tuchman, G. (1974). *The TV establishment: programing for power and profit*. Englewood Cliffs, NJ: Prentice-Hall.

Turkle, S. (1984). *The second self: Computers and the human spirit*. New York: Simon & Schuster.

TV, Hollywood square off on Fin-Syn. (1989, June 12). *Broadcasting*, p. 61.

TV makers forecast 9 percent dip in '79 sales. (1978, December 25). *Television Digest*, p. 7.

TV network ratings fall. (1989, June 28). *New York Times*, p. C22.

TV tape ready: CBS to use it next fall. (1956, April 14). *Television Digest*, p. 4.

TV that competes with the office grapevine. (1977, March 14). *Business Week*, pp. 49, 51, 54.

TV Digest. (1960). *TV factbook* (Fall/Winter ed., no. 31). Pennsylvania: Triangle Publications.

TV factbook. (1965, 1969, 1974, 1980). No. 35 (1965 ed.); Services volume, no. 39 (1969–1970 ed.); Services volume, no. 44 (1974–1975 ed.); Services volume, no. 49 (1980 ed.). Washington, DC: TV Digest, Inc.

Two-head color VTR. (1961, January). *Japan Electronics*, p. 21.

$250 VHS coming? (1984, June 11). *Television Digest*, p. 16.

Two made in Europe. (1964, October 5). *Television Digest*, p. 9.

Two more VTRs. (1966, February 14). *Television Digest*, p. 12.

Vandermeer, A. (1943). *The economy of time in industrial training: An evaluation study of the integrated use of certain United States Office of Education training films*. Ph.D. dissertation, University of Chicago, Chicago.

"The VCR future" seminar: Slowdown of home video growth seen by the end of decade. (1987, April 20). *Home Video Publisher*, p. 4.

VCR growth still reminiscent of color. (1982, February 1). *Television Digest*, p. 13.

VCR share survey shows major realignment. (1984, March 12). *Television Digest*, p. 12.

VCR penetration breaks 70% barrier. (1990, May 16). *Variety*, p. 35.

VCRs, people-meter: Factors in TV viewing. (1988, January 1). *Los Angeles Times*, sec. 6, p. 1.

VCR users do without ads: Study. (1983, October). *Advertising Age*, p. 10.

VHS gaining in VTR format battle. (1978, March 20). *Television Digest*, p. 9.

VHS 71, Beta 28. (1979, July 9). *Television Digest*, p. 11.

VHS's 3rd speed for six hours. (1979, April 23). *Television Digest*, p. 7.

Video cassettes pushing books off shelves. (1988, February 22). *New York Times*, sec. C, p. 13.

Video disc battle-lines firmly drawn. (1975, March 4). *Television Digest*, pp. 7–8.

The videoplay report. (1973, July 2). pp. 1–4.

Videoplayers—twenty systems in search of a market. (1970, July 20). *Television Digest*, p. 7.

Video recorder becomes consumer product. (1965, July 5). *Television Digest*, p. 8.

Videotape—A silver celebration—reunion. (1981, June 16). Program, New York Hilton Hotel, Trianon Ballroom.

Videotape gets new trick. Special report.

Video tape movies tested by the airlines. (1964, June 1). *Television Digest*, p. 7.

VTR's breaking and entering the home market. (1977, October 24). *Broadcasting*, p. 28.

What's new in video distributions. (1989, April 23). *New York Times*, p. F19.

Winslow, K. (1976). What's ahead for the videocassette/cartridge format. *Educational and Industrial Television, 12*, 29–32.

Winston, B. (1986). *Misunderstood media*. Cambridge, MA: Harvard University Press.

Zenith sets fall rollout for Betasystem. (1977, May 16). *Advertising Age*, pp. 1, 115.

Index

About the Authors

EUGENE MARLOW has been involved with media for over twenty-five years—as a marionetteer, stage manager, radio producer and announcer, author, scriptwriter, musician and composer, stage, film, and television producer/director, and educator. He is founder/president of Media Enterprises, a New York–based television and radio production and consulting company. A sister company, ME/II Productions, produces programing for domestic and international broadcast/home video markets.

Marlow has received dozens of awards for programing excellence from a variety of national and international organizations. He is also the author of and contributing author to several books on media and has published over eighty articles on broadcast television programing and video technologies in the United States and Europe.

Marlow received a Ph.D. in media studies from New York University in 1988 and an MBA from Golden Gate College in 1972. He teaches electronic journalism and business communications at Baruch College (City University of New York).

EUGENE SECUNDA (Ph.D., New York University) is an assistant professor in the Department of Marketing of Baruch College (City University of New York) and heads his own consulting company, Secunda Marketing Communications, in New York City. Prior to joining the

Baruch faculty, he was a visiting professor of marketing at New York University's Graduate School of Business Administration. He is also a contributing writer for *New York Magazine* and other publications in the media and marketing industries. Previously, Secunda was president of Barnum/Secunda Associates, an advertising/public relations agency. He also served in senior managerial posts at N.W. Ayer International and J. Walter Thompson Company advertising agencies. He began his career as a newspaper and radio reporter in the United States and in Europe.